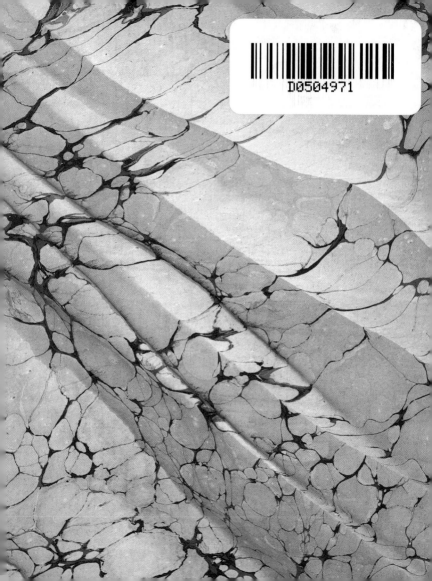

THE NATIONAL TRUST
Little Library

NUTS

JILL NORMAN

DORLING KINDERSLEY
LONDON

A DORLING KINDERSLEY BOOK

EDITOR LAURA HARPER

SENIOR EDITOR CAROLYN RYDEN

DESIGN MATHEWSON BULL

PHOTOGRAPHER DAVE KING

FIRST PUBLISHED IN GREAT BRITAIN IN 1990 BY
DORLING KINDERSLEY LIMITED
9 HENRIETTA STREET, LONDON WC2E 8PS

BRITISH LIBRARY CATALOGUING IN PUBLICATION DATA

NORMAN, JILL
NUTS
1. FOOD. NUTS
I. TITLE II. SERIES
641.345

ISBN 0-86318-489-8

PRINTED AND BOUND IN HONG KONG
BY IMAGO

C O N T E N T S

INTRODUCTION

*I*N THE WEST *we consume large quantities of nuts, usually roasted and salted, while having a drink, or as a snack between meals. Green almonds, fresh walnuts and cob nuts may still be offered with a glass of sweet wine at the end of a leisurely meal – a practice that goes back to antiquity.*

We have never regarded nuts as a serious part of our diet, although we are now more conscious of their protein, fat and mineral content. However, in other parts of the world nuts are an essential element in the diet, often used to supplement vegetable protein when meat or fish is not available or too expensive.

From West Africa across to Ethiopia, peanuts predominate. Roasted and ground, they are a constant ingredient in soups and stews. In Malay and Indonesian cooking a rich peanut sauce accompanies satay *(small skewers of grilled meat).*

In southern India cashews and coconut come into their own. Fried or toasted cashews are considered a delicacy when added to vegetable dishes, while all parts of the coconut make a contribution to the economy. In the north almonds and pistachios, two nuts once much favoured by the Mogul emperors, are still widely used. Slivered or ground, toasted or plain, they are found in pilafs, in delicately spiced savoury dishes of chicken or meat, and in puddings.

The Persians and Arabs use ground nuts – almonds, hazelnuts, walnuts or pistachios – to add body and flavour to long-cooked meat dishes, and to make rich sauces for poultry. The Arabs and Turks are masters of varied pastries filled with chopped nuts, and drenched in honey. Pine nuts, the delicately flavoured seeds of the Mediterranean stone pine, are added to rice dishes, stuffings, jams and sweetmeats.

Further west, around the Mediterranean, pine nuts are still more common; all the regions of Italy have specialities using pine nuts – with marinated sardines in Venice, spinach in Rome, swordfish in Sicily and to make pesto in Genoa. In Spain every small grocer sells pine nuts and they are cooked with rabbit, or chicken, added to sauces for fish or made into sweetmeats. In northern Europe almonds, hazelnuts and walnuts are the main nuts used in baking. Chestnuts can be bought roasted on street corners in autumn, but they also make excellent desserts and vegetable dishes.

French chestnut purée label, c. 1930

North America is the home of the pecan, once described as 'a walnut in a torpedo', a good nut for desserts and confectionery. Other nuts are cultivated widely in the United States, particularly almonds, walnuts, pistachios and peanuts.

Nuts are certainly one of our most versatile foods and in Western cooking their possibilities are often underrated. The recipes in this little book come from all parts of the world to tempt you to increase your repertoire of dishes in which nuts can be used.

ALMOND

*T*HE ALMONDS WE EAT *are the fruit of* Prunus amygdalus *(var.* dulcis*) which probably originated in the Near East but has long been grown throughout the Mediterranean region, including North Africa, and in other warm (but not tropical) zones from Kashmir to California and southern Australia. The Moguls adored them, so did the Romans. Their universal popularity has made them the dominant nuts in world trade, with Italy, Spain and California being the main exporters.*

Whole almonds

Almonds in their skin   *Blanched and peeled almonds*

Almonds are the most important nuts in gastronomy. Many go into baking and confectionery (from Bakewell tarts to marzipan). Oriental countries use them with rice (pilafs or stuffings), with poultry or meat – the West with fish. Ground almonds flavour and thicken soups and sauces. Almonds are added to salads and savoury dips. Real almond essence is made from bitter almonds (var. *amara*), which also flavour ratafias and macaroons.

Almond flakes

Sugared almonds

Coarse ground almonds

HAZELNUT

*M*ANY SPECIES *of hazelnut grow wild in temperate Asia, Europe and America, but only three are cultivated:* Coryllus avellana, *the cobnut of the Old World's temperate zones,* C. maxima, *the filbert of the Mediterranean region, overlapping in the Middle East with* C. colurna, *the Turkish hazel. Filberts have husks that extend well beyond the nut, cobs do not – but once they are shelled they are hard to tell apart, except that the Turkish hazel is smaller than the others. North America now cultivates only the* avellana *species.*

Hazelnuts have long been used as a raw food, gathered in the wild since mesolithic times, and found in the stores of Bronze Age settlements. Now the most important exporters are Italy, Spain, Turkey, France and northwest Africa. Other countries grow them for home consumption only.

Hazelnut oil

Filberts

Hazelnuts

Most nuts are eaten fresh, used in cakes and confections such as the various *tortone* (Italian nougats), or made into *gianduia* paste for fillings. Very young, fresh hazelnuts are good in salads – so is hazelnut oil.

Only Spain has created an extensive and inventive cuisine based on the hazelnut, culminating in the many versions of *salsa romesco*.

WALNUT

*T*HE WALNUT, Juglans regia, native to the temperate zone of Europe and Asia, has long been introduced to similar climates all over the world. Ancient Greece and Rome held it in esteem for its timber as well as its fruit, but the tree did not reach Britain until the 15th century. France, where walnuts are known just as 'nuts', is the main producer, closely followed by California and Oregon, Italy and Romania. China's large crop is used entirely in the home market.

Walnuts

Green walnuts

The large American black walnut, *J. nigra*, hard to crack and not as good to eat as the European varieties, is used mainly for flavouring, while the white walnut or butternut, *J. cinerea*, finds its way into confectionery. The unripe green fruit can be made into pickles or preserved in syrup. John Evelyn praised its use as a salad. Fresh 'wet' walnuts are a delicacy. Fully ripe nuts are eaten as dessert ('across the walnuts and the wine' – Tennyson) and used in baking and confectionery. Walnut oil makes fine dressings for salads and pasta, and also goes into artists' paint.

BRAZIL NUT

*B*RAZIL NUTS, *as the name suggests, originated in South America. The giant* Bertholettia excelsa *tree grows in the tropical forests of the Amazon region and produces fruit as large as a man's head, weighing several pounds and holding up to two dozen of the hard three-sided nuts, clustered together like segments of an orange. Although sporadically grown elsewhere, most nuts are still gathered in the wild in both Brazil and Venezuela.*

The Brazil nut, and even more so its close relation the sapucaya (*Lecythus zabucajo*), is underrated and little used – perhaps because it is hard to crack and, once cracked, goes rancid quickly since it is 65 percent oil. The nuts often substitute well for almonds and are very easy to grate or grind.

Shelled Brazil nuts

Brazil nuts

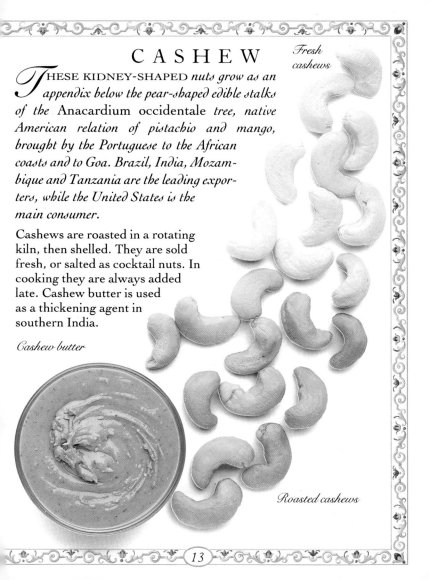

CASHEW

Fresh cashews

*T*HESE KIDNEY-SHAPED *nuts grow as an appendix below the pear-shaped edible stalks of the* Anacardium occidentale *tree, native American relation of pistachio and mango, brought by the Portuguese to the African coasts and to Goa. Brazil, India, Mozambique and Tanzania are the leading exporters, while the United States is the main consumer.*

Cashews are roasted in a rotating kiln, then shelled. They are sold fresh, or salted as cocktail nuts. In cooking they are always added late. Cashew butter is used as a thickening agent in southern India.

Cashew butter

Roasted cashews

PEANUT

*T*HE PEA *that poses as a nut*, Arachis hypogaea *of the* Leguminosae *family, stems from South America, but wherever it occurs these days (and that is in almost every subtropical region) it was planted by man. The Portuguese took it to West Africa, from where much later it was taken to North America, to Goa, from where it spread through India, and to the East Indies. China and India are the main producers now, but their entire crop is used at home – the rest of the world imports peanuts mostly from West Africa, especially Nigeria.*

Peanuts

Shelled peanuts

Peanuts are important
ingredients in West African
cooking, especially as a roasted
meal used to thicken soups and stews.
In Malaysia and Indonesia peanut paste forms
the base for *satay* sauces and for a dressing
for vegetables called *gado gado*.

Crunchy peanut butter

Salted peanuts

In the Western world peanuts have many uses. Roasted, they are salted as cocktail snacks or ground into peanut butter – used on its own or for cooking. Many confections with peanut are popular (peanut brittle, sugar- or chocolate-coated peanuts). The oil, known as groundnut oil, can be used for cooking and on salads.

Groundnut oil

COCONUT

*T*HE TALL Cocos nucifera *palm grows on every tropical shore, but its place of origin is obscure. It fruits throughout the year, making it a steady supplier of many necessities: fibre from the husk for rope and mats, the half shells as utensils, the flesh eaten fresh or dried. The dried flesh, known as copra, yields an oil much used for cosmetics and margarine. The Philippines and Indonesia are its main exporters, but many small Pacific islands depend on coconuts too.*

Coconut milk, pressed from the flesh macerated in water, is essential to the cuisine of Indonesia and Malaysia as the main thickening agent. It is also used in West Africa and on the 'slave coasts' of Colombia and Brazil to cook a rich and flavourful rice, and in India for sauces called *molee*. Desiccated coconut is the main form used in Western baking.

It can be soaked to make coconut milk but coconut cream is better and easier.

Coconut cream

Coconut

Grated fresh
coconut

Desiccated
coconut

CHESTNUT

*T*HE SWEET CHESTNUT, Castanea sativa, *is a native of southern Europe which has long become popular in other temperate zones for its timber as well as its nuts. The Romans may have brought the tree to Britain, much as early settlers took it to North America, where the native* C. dentata *has perished in a blight. The Japanese* C. crenata *and several other varieties are also edible.*

Chestnuts

Shelled chestnuts

Chestnuts are the only nuts to be treated as a vegetable: they contain much starch and little oil. Ground, they make good flour, but not for bread: it lacks gluten.

Peeled chestnuts

Both the husk and the brown skin of the nut must be taken off before the nuts are ready for further use.

Marrons glacés

Whole chestnuts

Boiled or roasted, ground or puréed or whole, chestnuts go into soups, stews, stuffings and desserts. *Marrons glacés* are chestnuts poached in syrup.

Chestnut purée

PINE NUT

THE NUTS of many pine trees are sought-after delicacies in countries as far apart as northern India (chilgoza), Chile (the monkey puzzle) and the American southwest, where Indians still gather the piñons *of the two-leaved pine. Only* Pinus pinea, *the stone pine, which grows wild from Portugal to the Black Sea, is cultivated for commerce.*

In the Middle East, pine nuts go into sweetmeats, stuffings and pilafs. Italy and Spain prefer them with vegetables and as a thickening for sauces such as *pesto* (from Genoa, which has an inventive pine nut cuisine). Also popular are chocolate-coated nuts and American *piñon* cookies.

Chopped pine nuts

Pine nuts

PISTACHIO

*P*ISTACIA VERA, *native to central Asia, reached the Mediterranean via the Near East, brought to Rome from Syria in the 1st century. It thrives on poor rocky soil in Iran, Greece, Turkey and the American southwest. As the harvested nuts are dried, their shells gape open and make the kernel easily accessible. Their natural colour is tan, but the shells are often dyed red. The nut is light green.*

Shelled pistachios

Pistachio nuts

In Western cooking these 'nuts of paradise' of the Mogul emperors are used mostly to decorate, but in the Middle East they are important ingredients. Whole nuts provide colour, taste and texture in many sweetmeats and stuffings. Pistachio ice cream well deserves its fame, as do salted cocktail pistachios.

PECAN

*T*HE Carya illinoensis *produces the pecan, best of the many edible hickory nuts, the native American answer to the walnut. They are usually sold in the shell (which is thin and easy to crack) because their high oil content of 70 percent makes them go rancid quickly. Pecans are cultivated only in the United States, below latitude 40° North, where the cotton and maize belts provide their favourite climate.*

A dessert nut, plain or salted, the pecan is equally good in baking or confectionery, notably pecan pie and brownies.

Shelled pecans

Pecans

MACADAMIA &
CANDLENUT

*T*HE MACADAMIA NUT (Macadamia ternifolia), *also known as Queensland nut from its origin in the forests of the northeastern Australian coast, is cultivated and exported on a large scale only on Hawaii.*

Macadamia nuts

Macadamias are among the nuts with a high oil content, prone to going rancid quickly. They are exported in vacuum packs to be eaten raw, roasted for dessert or salted as a cocktail snack. Few are used in confectionery.

Candlenuts

The tropical candlenuts, or kemiris, from *Aleurites moluccana*, are purgative when raw but safe once cooked. The shell is hard to crack, so the nuts are often broken. They are an essential ingredient in Indonesian and Malay cooking, for thickening soups and giving flavour to *sambals*.

Recipes

*All the recipes will serve 4,
but some (such as snacks and pastries)
will serve more*

SALTED ALMONDS

*¹/₂ egg white
1 lb/500 g unblanched almonds
4 teaspoons coarse sea salt*

Beat the egg white until it starts to froth. Put the nuts in a large bowl, pour over the egg white and turn the nuts in it with your hands to coat them evenly. Oil two baking sheets, spread the nuts on them and sprinkle with the salt, turning the nuts to coat them. Bake in a preheated oven, 120°C/250°F/gas ¹/₂, for 30 minutes. Shake the trays a few times to stop the nuts sticking. Turn off the heat and leave the nuts in the cooling oven for 30 minutes longer. When completely cool, store in an airtight container.

GLAZED WALNUTS

8 oz/250 g walnuts
4 oz/125 g sugar
4 fl oz/125 ml water
1 tablespoon oil
pepper (optional)

Put the nuts in a bowl, cover with boiling water and leave to stand for 30 minutes to remove any bitterness. Meanwhile make a syrup with the sugar and water. Drain the nuts and stir them into the syrup. Bring back to the boil and simmer for 3 minutes, then remove the pan from the heat and leave the nuts to absorb the syrup for 3–4 hours.

Heat the oil in a large frying pan or wok. Drain the nuts thoroughly, grind black pepper over them if you wish, and add them to the pan. Toss to coat them well with the oil and fry over medium heat, turning and stirring all the time or they will stick together. Cook for 3–4 minutes, then remove the nuts from the pan, separate any that stick together and leave to cool. Serve cold with drinks.

Variation

Glazed cashews can be prepared in the same way, but it is not necessary to blanch the nuts first.

PEANUT AND CUCUMBER SALAD

A simple spicy salad based on an
Indian recipe.

1 cucumber
1 small green pepper
*2 oz/50 g roasted peanuts, ground
coarsely*
*1 tablespoon fresh grated coconut
(optional)*
*2 tablespoons chopped mint
juice of ½ lemon*
1 teaspoon sugar
salt
2 tablespoons oil
½ teaspoon black mustard seeds
½ teaspoon cumin seeds
a pinch of cayenne

Peel and seed the cucumber and
cut into small dice. Remove the
seeds from the pepper and dice
it. Put the vegetables, nuts and
mint in a serving bowl. Stir the
lemon juice and sugar together,
add salt to taste and pour over.
Mix well. Heat the oil in a frying
pan, add the mustard seeds and
when they start to pop, add the
cumin and cayenne. Stir well
and when the spices darken
pour the mixture over the salad.
Toss and serve.

OLIVE, POMEGRANATE AND WALNUT SALAD

This salad is a speciality of Gaziantep in
southeastern Turkey, a town
surrounded by groves of olive,
pomegranate and nut trees.

2 large pomegranates
*4 oz/125 g green olives, stoned and
chopped*
a bunch of coriander, chopped
6–8 spring onions, chopped
4 oz/125 g walnuts, chopped coarsely
3 tablespoons olive oil
1½ tablespoons lemon juice
red pepper
salt

Cut open the pomegranates and
extract the seeds. Combine with
the olives, coriander, spring
onions and walnuts. Make a
piquant dressing with the
remaining ingredients, toss the
salad and serve. A few shredded
young sorrel leaves make a
pleasant addition.

Pumpkin and Chestnut Soufflé

1 lb/500 g pumpkin purée
(see below)
2 oz/50 g butter
¼ teaspoon ground cinnamon
¼ teaspoon ground ginger
salt and pepper
8 oz/250 g dried chestnuts,
soaked overnight
3 egg yolks
4 egg whites

To make pumpkin purée, cut a small pumpkin in half, remove the seeds and fibres, brush the flesh with a little melted butter or oil and bake in a preheated oven, 200°C/400°F/gas 6, for 15–20 minutes. Scoop out the flesh and purée it with the butter, spices, salt and pepper.

Cook the chestnuts in fresh water until tender – 45–60 minutes, depending on how old they are. Drain and then remove any bits of tough inner skin from the nuts and chop or grind quite finely. Stir into the pumpkin purée. Separate the eggs; stir the yolks into the vegetable purée. Whisk the whites until they form peaks, and fold them in as lightly as possible. Pour the mixture into a buttered 2 pint/1.2 litre soufflé dish and bake in a preheated oven, 200°C/400°F/gas 6 for 20 minutes, when the soufflé should be well risen and just set in the middle.

TROPICAL CRAB SALAD

12 oz/375 g white crab meat
1 papaya
1/2 small melon
1 avocado
salad leaves
3 oz/75 g macadamia nuts, chopped
5 tablespoons sunflower oil
2 tablespoons lemon juice
1 teaspoon grated lemon zest
1/4 teaspoon dry mustard
salt and pepper

Flake the crab meat. Cut the papaya, melon and avocado into cubes. Arrange the salad leaves on plates or in a bowl, put the crab and fruit on top. Scatter the nuts over the salad. Make a dressing with the remaining ingredients, spoon it over the salad and serve.

LEEKS WITH GARLIC AND BRAZIL NUTS

1 lb/500 g leeks, sliced
1 oz/25 g butter
2 cloves garlic, crushed
1 tablespoon lemon juice
2 teaspoons Kashmiri or other curry paste
3 oz/75 g Brazil nuts, grated coarsely

Cook the leeks in the butter in a heavy pan for 10 minutes, then add the other ingredients. Cover, cook for a further 5–10 minutes and serve. The leeks go well with lamb and with potatoes baked in their jackets.

BARLEY WITH CASHEWS AND BRUSSELS SPROUTS

2 oz/50 g butter
2 onions, sliced
8 oz/250 g pearl barley
1¼ pints/750 ml stock
4 oz/125 g cashews, chopped
salt and pepper
8 oz/250 g small Brussels sprouts

Melt half the butter in a casserole and stew the onions until soft. Stir in the barley and cook for a few minutes to coat it well with butter. Heat the stock and add it together with the cashews. Season, cover the casserole tightly and put it into a preheated oven, 180°C/350°F/gas 4, for about 45 minutes, until the barley is almost cooked and most of the liquid is absorbed.

Cook the Brussels sprouts in boiling water until almost soft, then drain them and toss in the remaining butter. Stir them into the barley and cashews, and return the casserole to the oven for a further 20–30 minutes.

SPINACH WITH PINE NUTS AND RAISINS

1½ lb/750 g spinach
3 tablespoons raisins
2 tablespoons olive oil
2 oz/50 g butter
2 cloves garlic, chopped
3 tablespoons pine nuts
salt, pepper and nutmeg

Wash the spinach and remove any large stalks. Drain and put it into a pan with the water that clings to it and cook, turning occasionally, until it has cooked down. Put the raisins to soak in warm water for a few minutes. Drain the spinach, squeeze out all the excess water and cut it into strips.

Heat the oil and butter in a large pan and fry the garlic until golden, then add the spinach, drained raisins and pine nuts. Season and cook for 5 minutes.

Dendeng

Dendeng is an Indonesian dish of spiced beef cooked in a little liquid until it is absorbed and the texture of the meat becomes soft but dry.

12 oz/375 g lean beef
6 candlenuts
10 shallots, chopped
3 cloves garlic, chopped
1 teaspoon ground galangal
1 teaspoon coriander
1/2 teaspoon cumin
4 tablespoons desiccated coconut
2 tablespoons oil
1 piece lemon grass, bruised
grated rind of 1 lemon
salt
4–6 tablespoons water

Cut the meat into very thin, small strips. Roast the candlenuts in a dry frying pan for a few minutes, then blend them with the shallots, garlic and spices. Mix with the coconut and coat the meat thoroughly. Heat the oil and fry the meat mixture until golden brown. Add the lemon grass, lemon rind and salt to taste, and the water. Cook very slowly for about an hour until the meat is soft and quite dry. Check from time to time that it is not sticking and, if necessary, add a little more water.

INDIAN GREEN BEANS
WITH COCONUT

1 lb/500 g green beans
2 oz/50 g fresh grated coconut
3 tablespoons chopped parsley
1 green chilli, seeded and chopped
2 tablespoons dry roasted
sesame seeds
salt
¼ teaspoon turmeric
2 tablespoons oil
1 tablespoon black mustard seeds

Top and tail the beans and cut
them into short pieces. Mix well

together the coconut, parsley,
chilli and sesame seeds, and put
the mixture aside. Cook the
beans until almost tender in
salted boiling water flavoured
with the turmeric. Heat the oil in
a frying pan, put in the mustard
seeds and when they start to pop
put in the drained beans. Cook
for 2–3 minutes, then stir in the
coconut mixture, remove from
the heat and serve.

LIVER SAUTÉED
WITH SHERRY AND HAZELNUTS

1 onion, sliced
2 cloves garlic, sliced
olive oil
1 lb/500 g calf's liver
flour
a small glass of dry sherry
salt and pepper
a handful of toasted hazelnuts,
chopped
a handful of parsley, chopped

Heat a little olive oil and sauté
the onion and garlic until

golden. Remove them from the
pan. Cut the liver into thin
slices, coat it in flour and fry
quickly on both sides, adding a
little more oil to the pan if
necessary. Return the onion and
garlic to the pan, add the sherry
and season with salt and pepper.
Stir in the nuts and parsley,
cook for a further 2 minutes
and serve.

CHICKEN WITH CASHEWS

2 tablespoons dry sherry
1 tablespoon cornflour
1 egg white
salt
1 lb/500 g chicken breast, cubed
2 tablespoons hoisin sauce
1 tablespoon soy sauce
2 teaspoons sesame oil
2 tablespoons oil
2 red peppers, seeded and cut in cubes
4 oz/125 g mushrooms, quartered
1 clove garlic, chopped
a small piece of fresh ginger, chopped
4 spring onions, sliced thinly
3 oz/75 g roasted cashews

Mix together 1 tablespoon of sherry with the cornflour, egg white and a little salt, and marinate the chicken for up to 2 hours. Combine the hoisin and soy sauces with the sesame oil and put the mixture aside. Heat a wok and put in the oil. When the oil is very hot, lower the heat and stir-fry the red peppers for 1 minute. Add the mushrooms, garlic, ginger and spring onions and fry for 30 seconds, then add the chicken. Raise the heat and toss well to cook the chicken. Pour in the sauce and cook for a further minute or so until the chicken is cooked through and coated with the sauce. Stir in the nuts for the last 30 seconds, and serve.

CHICKEN BRAISED IN WHITE WINE

1 chicken, cut in serving pieces
salt and pepper
flour
3 tablespoons olive oil
4 shallots, chopped
2 sprigs thyme
1 sprig marjoram
1 bay leaf
4 allspice berries
3 oz/75 g slivered almonds
4 new potatoes, peeled and quartered
a glass of dry white wine

Rub the chicken pieces with salt, pepper and flour, and sauté them in the oil until golden brown. Add all the other ingredients, cover the pan tightly and simmer over the lowest possible heat for about an hour, until the chicken is tender.

Variation
Use pine nuts instead of almonds.

FESENJAN

A rich Iranian dish of duck cooked in a walnut and pomegranate sauce. Chicken or pheasant can be used instead, if you wish.

1 duck, quartered
2 oz/50 g butter
2 onions, sliced
10 oz/300 g walnuts, ground
1 pint/600 ml water
salt and pepper
4 tablespoons pomegranate syrup
2 tablespoons sugar
2 tablespoons lemon juice
3 fl oz/75 ml water

Remove all excess fat from the duck and brown it lightly in the hot butter in a large casserole. Lift out the pieces and fry the onions until browned, then add the walnuts and 1 pint/600 ml water, and season with salt and pepper. Return the duck to the pan, bring the sauce to the boil, then cover and simmer for about 1 hour, until the duck is almost tender.

Stir the pomegranate syrup and sugar into the lemon juice and water. Skim as much fat as possible from the top of the sauce, then stir in the pomegranate mixture. If the sauce is too thick, add a little more water. Simmer for another 30 minutes until the sauce is quite dark. Serve with rice.

INDONESIAN PEANUT SAUCE

This sauce is excellent with satay (see below), rice or vegetables.

1 tablespoon groundnut oil
1 lb/500 g onions, chopped finely
1 clove garlic, chopped
1 teaspoon ground cumin
1/2 teaspoon ground ginger
6 oz/175 g peanut butter
2 tablespoons coconut cream
chilli powder
salt

Heat the oil in a heavy pan and add the onions, garlic, cumin and ginger. Stir well, turn the heat down very low and add the peanut butter and coconut cream. Cover and leave to cook for 2–3 hours. Stir occasionally to make sure it doesn't stick, and if necessary add a little water.

Eventually the sauce will become thick and smooth when stirred – you can put it through a food processor if you wish, but with long slow cooking this should not be necessary. Stir in chilli powder and salt to taste, cook for a further 10–15 minutes, and serve.

PORK SATAY

1 1/2 lb/750 g pork loin
a small piece of ginger, crushed
2 cloves garlic, crushed
1 teaspoon ground coriander
1 tablespoon groundnut oil
1/2 oz/15 g coconut cream soaked in
3 tablespoons water

Cut the pork into small cubes. Combine all the other ingredients in a blender to make a smooth marinade. Let the pork marinate for at least 2 hours, then thread the pieces onto small wooden skewers and grill for 5–6 minutes, turning as necessary. Serve with Indonesian peanut sauce.

ROMESCO SAUCE

This versatile Spanish sauce accompanies fish or shellfish, boiled vegetables and vegetable salads. In Spain it is made with the aromatic romesco pepper, but you can use a sweet red pepper and a pinch of cayenne instead.

1 dried romesco pepper or 1 sweet red pepper and a pinch of cayenne
4 cloves garlic, unpeeled
3 medium tomatoes
10 hazelnuts
10 almonds
1 tablespoon chopped parsley
2 tablespoons wine vinegar
3 fl oz/75 ml olive oil
salt and pepper

Remove the seeds from the romesco pepper and soak the pepper in water for 30 minutes. If using a fresh red pepper place this, with the garlic, tomatoes and nuts on a baking tray and put into a preheated oven, 200°C/400°F/gas 6. Remove the nuts after a few minutes when lightly toasted, the garlic and tomatoes when soft, and the pepper when the skin has blistered – it will take about 25 minutes. Peel all the vegetables; if you used a romesco pepper, drain it. Pound or process the nuts, garlic and pepper (and cayenne if using). Add the tomatoes and parsley and blend well. Beat in the vinegar and oil as if making mayonnaise, and add salt and pepper (and a little more cayenne if you wish). Leave at room temperature for at least 2 hours before serving.

Rice Pudding
WITH SAFFRON AND NUTS

This is very different from Western rice pudding; it has the consistency of a thick, rich cream.

3 oz/75 g long-grain rice
2 pints/1.2 litres milk
4 oz/125 g sugar
bruised seeds of 6 cardamoms
2 oz/50 g dried apricots, chopped
1/2 teaspoon saffron threads
1 tablespoon rose water
2 oz/50 g blanched almonds, chopped
2 oz/50 g pistachios, chopped

Wash the rice, bring the milk to the boil and stir in the rice. Cook over high heat for 1 minute, then turn the heat down very low and cook for a further 10 minutes, stirring all the time. Leave to cook slowly for 1 1/2 hours, stirring occasionally.

Add the sugar, cardamom and apricots and cook for a further 30 minutes, until the pudding thickens. Soak the saffron threads in the rose water for 20–30 minutes and stir them in with most of the nuts. Simmer for another 5 minutes, then pour the pudding into a shallow bowl. Sprinkle the remaining nuts over the top, and chill before serving.

Date and
WALNUT DESSERT

This dessert has its origins in the southern republics of the USSR, the region of the Caucasus mountains.

8 oz/250 g dates, chopped and stoned
4 oz/125 g walnuts, chopped
1/2 teaspoon ground cinnamon
2–3 tablespoons brandy

Put all the ingredients into a food processor or pound in a mortar until you have a fairly smooth texture. Spread the paste about 1/2 in/1 cm thick on a lightly oiled tray, cut into squares, and chill briefly. Excellent served with coffee.

Apricot and Pistachio Dessert

8 oz/250 g semi-dried apricots, chopped
4 oz/125 g shelled fresh pistachios, chopped
2–3 tablespoons rum

Put the apricots, pistachios and rum into the food processor or pound in a mortar to a rough purée. Spread to dry and cool as for *Date and walnut dessert*, opposite, and serve cut in squares.

Pistachio Shortbread

3 oz/75 g shelled pistachios
2 oz/50 g vanilla sugar*
5 oz/150 g plain flour
1/4 teaspoon baking powder
salt
4 oz/125 g butter

Heat the oven to 200°C/400°F/gas 6. Put the pistachios on a baking tray and toast them until they are just turning brown, about 6–8 minutes. Remove from the oven and leave to cool, then grind them finely with the vanilla sugar. Turn the oven down to 160°C/325°F/gas 3.

Sift together the flour, baking powder and a pinch of salt. Add the nut and sugar mixture and rub in the butter, gradually working the mixture to a stiff dough. Roll out on a floured surface to about 1/2 in/1 cm thick and cut into fingers or rounds. Put the shortbread on baking sheets and bake for 35–40 minutes, or until lightly coloured.

Variation

Replace the ground pistachios with ground almonds and mix with the sugar before adding to the flour.

*Vanilla sugar is made by keeping a vanilla pod in a jar of sugar, and topping up the sugar as you use it.

PECAN PIE

5 oz/150 g plain flour
salt
3 oz/75 g butter
1 egg yolk
2 tablespoons water
2 eggs
6 oz/175 g soft brown sugar
1 tablespoon flour
4 tablespoons milk
4 tablespoons melted butter
8 oz/250 g pecans, broken in pieces
1/4 pint/150 ml whipping cream
1 tablespoon icing sugar
1 tablespoon bourbon whisky

Make the pastry: add a pinch of salt to the flour, cut the butter into small pieces and rub it into the flour until it resembles coarse crumbs. Whisk the egg yolk with the water and blend into the flour mixture until it is smooth and forms a ball. Leave to rest for 5 minutes, then press with the hands to line a 9 in/23 cm tart tin. It is easier to pat the pastry over the bottom and sides of the tin than to roll it first, but make sure it is even and not too thick.

Beat the eggs lightly and whisk in the sugar, flour, milk and butter until smooth. Stir in the pecans and pour the filling into the pastry shell. Bake in a preheated oven, 220°C/425°F/gas 7, for 10 minutes, then lower the heat to 180°C/350°F/gas 4, and bake for a further 35–40 minutes. Serve warm or cold with whipped cream flavoured with the sugar and bourbon.

CHESTNUT DESSERT

1¹/₂ lb/750 g chestnuts
2 cloves
8 oz/250 g sugar
3 eggs
a few marrons glacés

Boil the chestnuts with the cloves, then peel and purée them in a vegetable mill. (If you prefer to omit this step you can use canned chestnut purée, with a little powdered clove added, but the taste will not be quite as good.) Beat together the sugar and egg yolks until pale and creamy, then stir in the chestnut purée. Beat the whites till they stand in peaks and fold them into the mixture.

Butter an ovenproof dish, such as a soufflé dish, and pour in the mixture. Cook in a preheated oven, 150°C/300°F/gas 2, for 45 minutes. When the dessert is cold, sprinkle the top with small pieces of marrons glacés and serve with cream.

ITALIAN CHESTNUT CAKE

This flat cake, made with chestnut flour, is a speciality of Florence. Chestnut flour can be bought from Italian shops and delicatessens.

3 tablespoons sultanas
8 oz/250 g chestnut flour
salt
3 tablespoons olive oil
3 tablespoons pine nuts
a sprig of rosemary

Soak the sultanas in warm water. Add a pinch of salt to the flour and 2 tablespoons of the oil, then a little at a time, add enough water (about ³/₄ pint/450 ml) to make a soft dough. Beat well and turn into an oiled shallow cake tin (9 in/23 cm in diameter). Drain the sultanas and scatter them over the top with the pine nuts and rosemary leaves. Sprinkle with the remaining oil and bake in a preheated oven, 190°C/325°F/gas 5, for about 50 minutes, or until the top is covered with a network of cracks. Cool in the tin on a rack.

INDEX

ACKNOWLEDGEMENTS

*The publishers
would like to thank
the following*

· TYPESETTING ·
TRADESPOOLS LTD
FROME

PHOTOGRAPHIC
· ASSISTANCE ·
JONATHAN BUCKLEY

JACKET
· PHOTOGRAPHY ·
DAVE KING

· ILLUSTRATOR ·
JANE THOMSON

· REPRODUCTION ·
COLOURSCAN
SINGAPORE

PAGE **5** RETROGRAPH ARCHIVE COLLECTION, LONDON

GWEN EDMONDS FOR ADDITIONAL HELP
KARL SHONE FOR PHOTOGRAPHY ON PAGES 6-7, 12-13

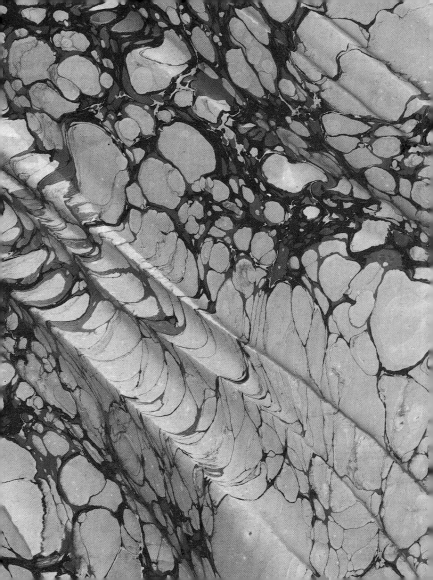

again, maybe the rich guy was a super sleuth. In which case, Alec understood. Sleuths had to keep a low profile. It was part of their job.

Dr. Glumsfeld had the annoying habit of always using long words that Alec didn't understand, like *apprehensive* and *perspicacity*. It made it very hard for Alec to figure out what he was talking about. He'd had the same problem yesterday.

"Oh, Officer Flint!" Dr. Glumsfeld said, walking very quickly to Alec's dad's side — his feet *swish-swished* too, kind of like Fernando-call-me-Frank's. "You wouldn't believe what happened! The sound that swelled from those alarm bells really was just too much. It made me quite apprehensive. I hope we can count on your perspicacity in this matter and that you'll find the thief instantaneously."

Officer Flint rolled his eyes at Alec. They had laughed about Dr. Glumsfeld the night before at dinner, Alec's dad saying things like, "Alexander, may I have another serviette?" instead of, "Hey, Al, can you pass me a napkin?" Alec tried too with, "May I please have some carbonated beverage?" But Officer Flint said, "Nice try, buddy." Soda was not allowed in the Flint house, except on special occasions. And a regular old Sunday night was *not* a special occasion.

While Alec's dad spoke to Dr. Glumsfeld, Alec wandered off and retraced the route he'd taken through the museum the day before. Only now he had to remember what the exhibit used to look like — to see what wasn't there. That would be the tricky part. Yesterday, he could just open his eyes and look at the different artifacts. Now he could only imagine. Alec closed his eyes and rubbed thoughts into his brain.

Yesterday the room had been packed. Alec Flint hadn't been able to look anywhere without seeing huge glass cases filled with books, or roped-off displays of cutlasses and broadswords. There had been chests and boxes that looked like they belonged in a pirate story, and a glass container that held a big pile of gold coins. Alec kept rubbing his head to remember more about the exhibit. He had looked at the gold coins for a long time yesterday and thought that they must've been worth three thousand dollars. Or maybe a million.

Alec wasn't sure how much gold or other jewelry stuff cost since he never bought any. The only jewelry he wore was the detective watch his mom got him the last time she went to San Francisco. It had buttons that let you set three different time zones, and a stopwatch, and it was glow-in-the-dark besides. But detective watches weren't really jewelry as far as Alec was concerned, and they certainly weren't made of gold. They were only sort of jewelry. The kind that was okay for a boy to wear without feeling girlie.

Alec opened his eyes and checked his detective watch. Still twenty minutes until school started. Alec read the plaque on the wall next to the case where the gold coins used to be. The perp hadn't taken the plaque. It said, *"These coins are part of the treasure Christopher Columbus brought on the* Niña *during his first voyage to America. Columbus planned on trading them for goods in the Indies."*

Officer Flint was still talking to Dr. Glumsfeld — Alec checked — so he kept wandering around the empty exhibit.

He remembered yesterday when he'd walked around with Emily Berg. She was there because her dad, Alfred Berg, was in charge of the insurance company in Laurel Hollows. As far as Alec knew, that meant if expensive things got stolen, Officer Flint had to find them fast, otherwise Emily's dad's company had to pay big bucks to whoever lost them. In this case, it would be the anonymous benefactor. Officer Flint got invited to things like the Christopher Columbus exhibit to keep an eye on what was

ALEC FLINT

SUPER SLEUTH

The Niña, the Pinta, AND THE Vanishing Treasure

BY JILL SANTOPOLO

ILLUSTRATIONS BY C.B. CANGA

ORCHARD BOOKS · NEW YORK

An Imprint of Scholastic Inc.

This book was originally published by Orchard Books in 2008.

ISBN-13: 978-0-545-06645-7

ISBN-10: 0-545-06645-X

12 11 10 9 8 7 6 5 4 3 2 1   8 9 10 11/0

Printed in China
This edition, first printing, September 2008

To Marilyn Wallace,
who inspired me to dream.
And to my parents, Beth and John
Santopolo, whose belief in me made
those dreams seem possible.

Chapter 1

Convenient Sweatshirt Pouches

Alec Flint looked down at his socks, trying to decide whether they were the sort of socks a super sleuth would wear. They were green. With black stripes. Black was a super-sleuthy color, as far as Alec was concerned. Green, not so much. But he liked it just the same.

"Alec!" his father yelled up the stairs.

"Almost ready!" Alec yelled back.

He slipped on his favorite green sweatshirt — it had a hood and a convenient pouch in the front where he could store things. Like his hands if they got cold. Or detective pens.

Alec owned one really good detective pen that could write even if you were holding it upside down. His mom got it for him when she went to Washington, D.C., a while back. Alec grabbed the pen off of his desk and put it in the sweatshirt pouch. You never knew when you'd need a good detective pen.

"Alec!" his father yelled again. "You don't want to miss the bus!"

But Alec didn't answer. He was too busy putting gel in his hair to make it spiky. Alec liked running his fingers back and forth over the hard spikes when he was thinking. It was like rubbing thoughts into his brain. While he was spiking, he heard the phone ring. Then his dad yelled up the stairs once more.

"Al! The station just called! I have to head back over to the museum! You've gotta come with me — now!"

Ooh, he was going to get to go on official police business!

"Coming!" Alec yelled downstairs.

Then he grabbed his backpack and crawled under his bed — somehow his sneakers always ended up there no matter where he remembered taking them off. Yup. There they were. Black. Size 3. Laces still in a double knot from the day before. Maybe his dad had stuck them under his bed while he was sleeping. Maybe his dad *always* stuck them under his bed while he was sleeping. Alec hadn't thought of that before, but it was possible. He might have to do a sneaker stakeout one night to see. That is, if no other more important super-sleuth cases came along first.

Alec slipped his feet into his sneakers and ran downstairs. He didn't make his bed. It was a deal he had with his dad. When Mrs. Flint was away on business and it was just the boys, no beds got made in the whole house. Not even if guests came.

When Alec got to the kitchen, his father handed him a baggie filled with Cap'n Crunch cereal. It was Alec's favorite. He loved eating the Cap'n Crunches one by one, chewing them up as quickly and quietly as he could. He figured that's how he would have to eat when he was on a stakeout — quickly and quietly — so he practiced whenever he was able.

Alec Flint and his father got into an unmarked vehicle — at least, that's what Officer Flint called it. It was a car that the police department gave him, but it wasn't a patrol car with flashing lights or anything. It *did* have a little light on the inside you could stick on the roof if you had to speed to chase a perp. Perp is what Officer Flint called a bad guy. Alec liked the word. *Perp.* He said it a few times in his head for fun.

✿✿✿

At the museum, Officer Flint and Alec walked through the big marble lobby they'd entered into the day before. They'd been there because Officer Flint was supposed to guard the Christopher Columbus exhibit. Which he'd done. Only, Alec learned in the car, once they'd left, a perp came and stole the entire thing.

Alec followed behind his father, trying to walk quietly. Super sleuths *always* did things quietly — at least, that's what Alec figured. But unfortunately, the hard marble floors of the museum were not made for sleuth-walking. Alec's sneakers *squeaked* and *squealed* and generally made a racket as he walked behind his father. Without even looking down, Alec knew that Officer Flint was not wearing sneakers — he was wearing his black shoes with the bottoms that *clip-clopped* as he walked.

You could tell a lot about people by the way their shoes sounded, Alec thought. His father's shoes sounded serious. His own shoes sounded noisy and kidlike... not the best sound for a super sleuth. Maybe he could get his dad to buy him some new shoes.

As Alec *squeaked* down the hallway, trying to make his sneakers sound sleuthier, he heard

a third pair of shoes. These shoes *swish-swished* on the ground. They sounded sneaky. And not like sneakers sneaky, like plain-old-sneaky sneaky. Alec couldn't even tell how close they were. *Swish-swish. Swish-swish. Pop!* A security guard popped up out of nowhere, right next to Officer Flint. Alec observed him. His name tag said FERNANDO, though he said to call him Frank, and he had come to escort Officer Flint to the room that formerly held the Christopher Columbus exhibit.

"Really a pity," Fernando said, and then started tugging on his collar. "Warm in this place, no?"

Alec's hands were shoved into his useful sweat-shirt pocket.

"Not to me," he said.

Fernando-call-me-Frank gave him a Look. Alec didn't even have to be a detective to know what that kind of Look meant: Fernando did not like

Alec Flint. And Alec Flint? He did not like Fernando.

Once they got to the exhibit room, Officer Flint and Alec were greeted by Dr. Glumsfeld, the curator of the American History Museum. Alec knew from his father that Dr. Glumsfeld was supposed to be very smart. And he was good at making rich people give money to the museum, which, according to Officer Flint, was very poor. In fact, Dr. Glumsfeld had told them yesterday that one of the rich people donated the whole Christopher Columbus exhibit from his own personal collection of artifacts. Only, Dr. Glumsfeld didn't call the guy a rich person — he called him an anonymous benefactor, which Officer Flint said really meant a rich guy who didn't want anyone to know who he was.

Alec Flint thought that was funny — if he were a rich guy and gave a whole entire exhibit to a museum, he'd want his name hanging on the door. In big letters. Preferably green. But then

happening. Alfred Berg was not invited, but came anyway.

Emily Berg was bouncy. She was also Alec's next-door neighbor. And in his same class at school. Alec Flint had been looking at the gold coins when Emily *squeak-squeal-bounced* over to him and said, "Hey, Alec, isn't this stuff cool?"

"Uh, yeah," Alec had said. "Totally."

It wasn't that Alec didn't like Emily — he liked her tons more than he liked Fernando the creepy security guard, for example — but sometimes he wished she would stop bouncing for a while. Even talking to her made him a little tired.

"I *love* going to museums like this, don't you, Alec? Don't you?" she had said, bouncing.

Alec did like going to museums like this, especially when the exhibits were on the FBI or old TV shows where people were police car partners. There was one exhibit he and his dad saw that was all about the old TV show named *Car 54,*

Where Are You? Alec liked how Officer Toody and Officer Muldoon got to be detectives together. Like a team. Alec thought, as he had on many occasions before, that it would be nice to find someone to be a detective team with him. But not Emily Berg. As far as Alec was concerned, Emily Berg would make a terrible sleuth. She wouldn't be quiet long enough to go on a stakeout or anything.

"I'm working for my dad today, Emily," he'd said to her yesterday. "I can't really talk."

"Oh!" Emily had said, her eyes wide. "Got it!" Then she'd zipped her lips — actually zipped them all the way across with her fingers — and, much to Alec's surprise, stood quietly next to him while he'd examined the exhibit and watched for perps.

After the gold, Alec had checked out a big leather-bound book in a glass case. He'd stood on his sneaker toes to see inside. The front cover hadn't said anything — it was just sort of brown and leathery. It had looked like someone made it out of an old, worn shoe.

Alec closed his eyes and rubbed some more thoughts into his brain so he could remember what the book was like when it was actually there, but he couldn't think of anything else, other than the shoe thing. So he opened his eyes and looked at the plaque that was still on the wall. It said: *"Captain's Log of Christopher Columbus."* And since you couldn't see inside the book — even before it had gone missing — because it was locked in the case, there were pictures stuck on the wall of what was inside. Alec glanced at the pictures, which were mostly just round, curly handwriting in another language, and kept going. He checked his watch again — Officer Flint was still talking to Dr. Glumsfeld, and there were fifteen minutes left until Alec had to get to school.

On the side of the next empty case, Alec read from a plaque that said: *"Part of the* Pinta's *Sail."* The air-conditioned box was still there, where the piece of *Pinta* sail had been stored so it wouldn't rot, but the fabric was gone. Alec wondered who had found this sail section and where the rest of the *Pinta* was. Maybe rotting somewhere at the bottom of the ocean. Alec secretly hoped so. He was not a fan of Christopher Columbus or his ships.

Alec moved on from the empty air-conditioned box to the empty stand where yesterday he and Emily had looked through the telescope that one of Columbus's men used to spy land. It hadn't been all locked up, and you could actually touch it. Yesterday, Alec had slid the wooden telescope in and out, making it longer and shorter. When he'd looked through the lenses, he'd seen Emily's eye up close.

"Can I try?" she'd asked.

"Sure," Alec had said.

After he'd handed it over, Emily had put one hand on her hip and twirled the telescope around like a baton in the other hand. Then she'd dropped it. The clatter had echoed through the big room. Alec had bent to pick up the telescope and had given it back to Emily.

"Good thing the piece you look through didn't break," he'd said, slightly worried that it wouldn't be shady characters who ruined the Christopher Columbus exhibit, but it would be Emily Berg.

After the clatter, Dr. Glumsfeld had *swish-swished* over and appeared next to Alec and Emily.

"I think it would be a wonderful idea if the two of you returned to your fathers," he'd said, and looked hard at Alec.

Emily Berg had stuck out her tongue behind Dr. Glumsfeld's back. Alec had not stuck out his tongue. He'd had the notion that Dr. Glumsfeld's idea was more an order than a suggestion and wanted to get away from him as quickly as possible. Alec had *squeak-squealed* back to his father. Emily had *squeak-squeal-bounced* back to hers.

And that's what Alec Flint did again because he realized that, according to his detective watch, he only had four minutes to get to school before the bell.

"Dad!" he whispered loudly to Officer Flint. "School!"

Officer Flint looked at his watch and his eyes popped open very wide. "Cripes!" he said, which Alec Flint knew meant his dad thought they were in trouble. He only said "cripes" when things got bad.

"Dr. Glumsfeld," Officer Flint said, "I'll be right back. Just have to take my son to school. If you'll fill out this missing-items report, I'll be back to go over it with you in a jiff."

"Of course!" Dr. Glumsfeld said.

Fernando-call-me-Frank escorted Alec and Officer Flint out of the museum. Alec spied on him as they walked. It looked like there was a bulge in the back of his pocket. A bulge the size of a gold coin. Alec looked over at his dad, but Officer Flint wasn't paying attention to Fernando.

Hmm, thought Alec, *this might be a case for a super sleuth.* He pulled his detective notebook out of his pocket and his pen out of his convenient sweatshirt pouch. Then Alec Flint began to write.

Chapter 2

Late Napkin Notes

Alec sat in his father's unmarked vehicle and thought about Christopher Columbus. The explorer was ruining his life. First he had to spend a whole Sunday in the museum with Emily Berg looking at the exhibit that got stolen, and then it made him late for school.

But even before the weekend, Alec had decided that he didn't like Christopher Columbus very much. He didn't like rhymes like "In fourteen hundred ninety-two, Columbus sailed the ocean blue." He didn't like the *Niña,* the *Pinta,* and the *Santa María.* Especially not the *Pinta.* What even *was* a Pinta? And above all, he didn't like the stories about Christopher Columbus giving Native Americans diseases like chicken pox. Or was it smallpox? Alec could never remember which, but he was certain it was a pox. And after sitting in a bath filled with oatmeal for a week when he was in kindergarten, Alec Flint knew how bad it was to have any kind of pox.

Besides, Alec had always been a big fan of Native American trackers. He read about them whenever he could, which was usually every Wednesday when his class had library right after lunch. Alec liked how the trackers followed animals so quietly that the animals didn't even know they were being hunted until — *bam!* — an arrow hit them right in the leg, or back, or shoulder, or whatever body part the hunter was aiming to hit. Those animals never even saw it coming.

Unfortunately, though, Alec Flint's feelings about Christopher Columbus did not faze his father, who kept taking him to the Christopher Columbus exhibit, or his teacher, Mrs. Jones, who assigned a report on C.C. This was all because Columbus Day was coming up and Mrs. Jones was taking the class on a field trip to the Laurel Hollows Columbus Day Parade. The parade was a sorry excuse for a field trip, according to Alec Flint, who would have rather gone to the fire-house, or the police station, or even to the park to watch an ant carry a crumb around the baseball diamond. It just proved that Alec couldn't escape dumb old Columbus.

Alec pulled out his detective notebook, which some-times doubled as an assignment pad —

but only when there were Very Important Things to do — and jotted down: *Write Columbus paper.* Then he added: *Also do research.* He'd forgotten for a second about the research part.

By the time Alec had finished writing in his detective notebook, Officer Flint had pulled up to the front of Laurel Hollows Elementary School East. That was Alec's school. And Alec got out of the car just as the bell was ringing. The late bell. Which meant he was going to be in big trouble unless he had a note. Which Officer Flint quickly wrote on a napkin and handed to Alec.

"Just give it to Mrs. Jones," Officer Flint said. "It'll be okay."

Alec stuffed the note into one of the useful pockets in his cargo pants. He loved pockets. Sometimes, in his detective notebook, Alec Flint made lists of things he could keep in his pockets when he was a super sleuth for real. Like magnifying glasses and flashlights and cameras to take pictures of evidence.

"Thanks, Dad," said Alec Flint. "See you after school."

"Sure thing, Al," Officer Flint said. "And if I'm not home by the time you get off the bus, just walk down to Mrs. McGrady's."

Alec groaned. One of the things Alec Flint hated more than Christopher Columbus was spending an afternoon with Mrs. McGrady. He'd done it before. More times than he'd like to remember. And it usually involved watching her knit teeny sweaters for her grandchildren and grandpets in other states while a boring show was on TV. It never involved going to the park, or riding his bike outside, or even playing video games. And it always involved staying at Mrs. McGrady's house down the block, which smelled of old cat and coffee and lemon-scented air freshener. Not a good smell combination as far as Alec was concerned. Though thankfully she had cats and not dogs. Alec Flint was *not* a fan of dogs.

Alec thought when he was a grown-up profes-
sional super sleuth, one of his cases might be to
find out if Mrs. McGrady's grandpets ever wore
the sweaters she knitted for them. He'd never
heard of pets wearing sweaters. If he were covered in fur, Alec Flint didn't think he'd want to
wear a sweater either. And anyway, he preferred
sweatshirts. With useful pockets. And hoods.

"Please be home," Alec said to his dad. "I hate
it there."

"I know, Al," said Officer Flint. "I'll try my
hardest. But just in case."

"Fine," Alec said. "Just in case."

And in a kind of grumpy mood, he walked
into Laurel Hollows Elementary School East to
give his late napkin note to Mrs. Jones.

In Mrs. Jones's class, Monday was art day.
Tuesday and Thursday were P.E., which stood for
Physical Education and really just meant playing

sports. Alec Flint secretly called it P.U. because the gym always smelled like sweaty socks and Cheez Doodles. Alec did not like sweaty socks or Cheez Doodles. But he liked P.E. And he liked it even better when they had P.E. outside, where it smelled like dirt and trees. Wednesday was library, and Friday was music. Those activities were called "specials."

Alec's teacher, Mrs. Jones, had the specials schedule written in big block letters on the bulletin board next to the door. She had the classroom schedule there too. In the morning, the bell rang at 8:03 — that was written in red and was the bell that Alec Flint had missed on account of being late because of the museum. People actually walked in after that bell a lot because the buses sometimes let kids off late, mainly because of traffic lights and kids forgetting things and holding up the bus. Then from 8:03 to 8:45 was Do Now time — that was written in blue.

When Alec handed Mrs. Jones his late napkin note, she nodded and told him to find his seat. Which he did. Then he unpacked his backpack and started the Do Now. The Do Now was always made up of brainteasers. "Time to wake up your brains!" Mrs. Jones said.

Alec pulled his favorite pencil out of his desk — it was black and skinny and could be hidden quickly in tiny spaces. Very useful for sleuths on the go. He left his special pen in his sweatshirt pouch. It was good for writing upside down, but not for erasing. And with the Do Now, Alec sometimes needed to do a lot of erasing. After Alec sharpened his black pencil, he looked up at the Do Now written on the board. It said:

> ### Riddle Me This:
> ### C had 3 S: the N, the P, and the SM.
> ### Math Madness: XXY–ZZZ=YYZ
> ### Rebus Riot: SHRIMP

The Rebus Riot was a piece of cake — it was so easy that Alec could do it as quickly as he could eat a whole slice of chocolate cake. Alec saw that the word *shrimp* was written really, really big. He knew that number three was always a common phrase written in a tricky way. Like last Friday it was the phrase "a stitch in time," but it was written like "TI*stitch*ME." The answer to this one was definitely "jumbo shrimp." Alec wrote that down on a piece of loose-leaf paper in his Do Now binder.

Then he looked at Riddle Me This. That was always a sentence with numbers included where you had to guess what the letters stood for, like "365 D in a Y" was "365 days in a year." Alec Flint looked at it for a second before he groaned. It was about Christopher Columbus. Alec wrote on his paper, "*Columbus had 3 ships, the* Niña, *the* Pinta, *and the* Santa María." As far as Alec Flint was concerned, Mrs. Jones was taking this Columbus Day field trip a little bit too far.

Then Alec got down to work. Math Madness always took him the longest. It was a math problem without numbers. He had to figure out which number each letter stood for. Days when he could figure out Math Madness were always good days for Alec Flint. He could get it about half the time. Emily Berg could never get Math Madness. But the new girl who sat next to Alec, Gina Rossi? She could *always* figure out Math Madness. And sometimes she figured out more than one way to get the math to work right. She was really good at math. And at mostly everything else, it seemed to Alec Flint.

Alec looked at the problem. He had a method where he started with easy numbers. This time he was going to use 1, 2, and 3. Sometimes he started with 0, 1, and 2, but this morning he felt like skipping 0. So for all the Y's he wrote "2" and for all the Z's he wrote "1." Then he did the math backward. Y+Z was 2+1, which equaled 3. So X was maybe 3. Then he tried the whole thing: 332−111=221. Yes! It worked! Alec had done it! He solved Math Madness! On his first try!

Alec was so happy that he sang the *Mission: Impossible* theme song. Quietly. In a whisper voice. Gina Rossi looked over to see what Alec was doing. Then she looked at Alec's paper.

"There are two other answers for Math Madness," she whispered.

Alec Flint stopped midsong. Just then Mrs. Jones said, "Okay, Do Now time is finished. Let's go over the answers."

Alec didn't say anything back to Gina. He didn't really know her very well. She went to the other elementary school in Laurel Hollows — West — up until two weeks ago when her parents moved across town and she got switched into his class, right next to his seat. Alec Flint thought she looked a little bit like Princess Jasmine from the *Aladdin* movie, but he never said that out loud. Though, when he did a stakeout on her in class, he sometimes gave her the code name of P.J. in his head.

Mrs. Jones started going over the right answers. When she got to the answers for Math Madness, Gina raised her hand. She was the only one who had gotten all three answers. Alec looked at Gina's paper as she said the answers out loud: "It's 332 minus 111 equals 221. And 664 minus 222 equals 442. And also 996 minus 333 equals 663."

Alec was impressed. P.J. was smart. Really smart. *She* would make a super-good sleuth. Maybe even the perfect police car partner. She could be in charge of math things. And maybe other things too. It was definitely worth considering.

After the Do Now came a math lesson. Mrs. Jones was teaching times. Like, anything times zero equals zero. And anything times one equals itself, whatever that anything was. Alec Flint got it pretty quickly and yelled, "Nine!" along with some other people in the class, including Gina, when Mrs. Jones asked what nine times one was.

While Mrs. Jones kept explaining about the one times table to people like Emily Berg who were having some trouble, Alec Flint staked out Gina a little more. She was writing something on her math paper that wasn't math at all. It was words. But not any words that Alec could read. It said:

Wvzi Zoovtiz,

Nb xozhh rh hlll ylirmt.*

Alec spent the rest of the math lesson trying to figure out what Gina was writing and what a Zoovtiz was. He didn't pay attention to Mrs. Jones again until she clapped her hands and said, "I'm passing out a math worksheet for homework. Once you've put your worksheet in your homework folder, please line up in two single-file lines so we can walk quickly and quietly to art."

Emily Berg, who sat in front of Alec, passed the math worksheets back to him. He took one and passed the rest to Emily's best friend, Carrie Leff, who sat behind him. Then he put the

34

worksheet in his homework folder and lined up as directed. Emily and Carrie did not line up as directed. They stood by Alec's desk and compared their headbands. Then they traded. Alec observed them from his place in line.

While he was observing, he felt a tug on the sleeve of his hooded sweatshirt. It was Gina. "Hey," she whispered. "I saw you looking at the note I was writing my sister in our secret code. Sit next to me in art and I'll teach it to you too."

Alec thought this might be a nice way to test how good P.J. would be as a police car partner. Plus he figured he needed to learn as many secret codes as possible so he would know them for his future jobs — just in case there was a perp who wrote clues in a secret code. Or if maybe he'd have to write one himself to give information to other sleuths. You never knew when you would need to write a coded note to someone.

So Alec whispered, "Okay," to Gina and then walked with the rest of his class quickly and quietly to art. Too late he realized that if Gina had seen him looking at her paper, it meant he was a bit of a crummy sleuth. He would have to work on that. Big-time.

Chapter 3

What's a Zoovtiz?

When they got to the door right outside of art, Mrs. Jones put up her hands and the whole class stopped. Quickly and quietly. It was like Mrs. Jones was training everyone to go on stakeouts.

Gina whispered to Alec Flint, "There's a sub today."

Alec Flint's eyes got big. How did she know that? Was Gina already a detective? And a better one than he was? Alec Flint *knew* he was going to miss out on things when his dad made him go to that dumb museum this morning.

"How do you know?" he asked her suspiciously.

"My sister," she whispered. "She had the sub on Friday. Said that Ms. Blume would be out today too. She's getting married at the big church down the street next Saturday or Sunday or something and had to prepare things for the wedding. But she left stuff for us to do."

"*Hmmm,*" Alec whispered back. He wasn't particularly interested in the sub or Ms. Blume's wedding. All his extra brain space was taken up by the missing Christopher Columbus exhibit. Could that really have been a gold coin in Fernando-call-me-Frank's pocket? Alec Flint had done a lot of practice sleuthing before — stakeouts on Emily Berg and P.J. and Mrs. McGrady knitting — but this was his first shot at figuring out something big. It was his chance to prove he could be a real honest-to-goodness detective.

When the art door finally opened and Mrs. Jones's class was allowed to go in, Alec Flint saw,

much to his dismay, that the sub was Ms. Levine. Alec did not like Ms. Levine. In fact, he once wrote a poem about her in his head that went: "Ms. Levine the submarine
is very loud and very
mean." Ms. Levine
liked to yell.
And she
yelled
very
loudly.
Always.
Even when she
was just talking,
she yelled her words.

"SIT DOWN," she yelled
the minute the door closed
behind the last students who
came into art. Everyone sat down,
including Alec Flint, who found
an empty chair next to Gina Rossi.

Ms. Levine kept talking very loudly. "We have a problem today, children. The art closet doors seem to be locked, and no one has a key except for Ms. Blume, who seems to be missing."

"*Are* they locked, or do they just *seem* to be locked?" Gina whispered to Alec Flint. "She's dumb if she doesn't know the difference."

Alec puzzled the difference out himself. "Yeah," he whispered to Gina. "She's dumb. The closets *are* locked, and I bet Ms. Blume *is* missing!"

"Someone seems to be talking on that side of the room," Ms. Levine said loudly, pointing to Alec and Gina's table.

"Actually," said Gina, "we *are* talking. We were wondering about where Ms. Blume is and why she locked the closet doors."

Alec Flint thought Gina was brave to stand up to Ms. Levine like that. Brave like detectives sometimes had to be brave. The more Alec knew about Gina, the more he thought she'd be a perfect police car partner.

"I don't *know* why she locked the doors, or where she went, Miss . . ."

"Rossi," Gina answered. "I'm new."

"Miss Rossi. I told you, she seems to be missing, along with the keys to the art closets. We've been calling her house and her cell phone all day, and we even sent a teacher over to her place earlier this morning. Her car seems to be missing too, but the teacher could hear a dog barking inside and scratching to get out. Her mail and newspapers have been there since Thursday, piling up. It's very strange. But, she's probably just caught up in wedding preparations. So, everyone, I have some paper and some pencils. You can . . . draw a picture. I'll be here if you need me. And *no* going to the bathroom more than one at a time."

Ms. Levine passed out the paper and pencils and sat down at Ms. Blume's desk.

"This is great," Gina said to Alec Flint. "Now I can show you the code."

But Alec Flint had his hand on top of his spiky hair and was rubbing thoughts into his brain. If he asked Gina to be his detective partner, that meant that he'd have to trust her one hundred percent on everything, for as long as they were partners. And once she *was* his partner, it would be hard to be un-partners... at least without hurting her feelings. Was she the kind of person he could trust? Could they be partners for a really long time? At least until the end of fourth grade? She seemed really smart and all, and nice too. And she knew secret codes... well, she knew at least one secret code....

"Alec?" Gina said.

"Sorry," said Alec. "I was just thinking about something." He looked around to make sure no one was listening. "See, the reason I want to learn your code is that I'm a super sleuth."

"Really?" said Gina, and her eyes got kind of brighter. "Like you get to track down criminals and find out about murders and stuff?"

Alec blushed. "Well, not yet," he admitted. "But I'm learning. Like, teaching myself how to be a super sleuth. I'm a super sleuth-in-training, really."

"Oh, that's cool too," said Gina. "What does a super sleuth do? I mean, other than catch criminals."

Alec was rubbing his hair furiously. "Well, there's that. And also, umm, going on stakeouts, and questioning witnesses, and wearing black . . ." Alec realized he wasn't making much sense. "And solving mysteries too," he said. "Important ones. That's why it's not just 'a sleuth' — why there's a 'super' in there first."

"Solving mysteries?" asked Gina. "Now *that's* really cool, because after coming to art today, I think I have a mystery to solve. An important one. Do you think you could be a super sleuth about my mystery?"

"Well," said Alec Flint, "I think I already have an important mystery to solve. It's about a missing Christopher Columbus exhibit at the museum. I'm helping my dad. But he's not a super sleuth — he's a police officer, which is sort of like a super sleuth but a little bit different."

"Oh, that's too bad," said Gina. "Because since I'm not training to be a super sleuth or anything, I don't know if I'll be able to solve my mystery myself." She shrugged. "I guess I can try, though."

Alec Flint was curious. He never knew a kid who had a mystery before.

"Well," he said, "maybe I can do both. What's your mystery?"

"Ms. Blume," Gina answered, "as in, where is she? I *know* the closets weren't locked on Friday because my sister made this ugly macaroni project with Ms. Levine and said that she kept having to go to the closet to look for the right kind of stupid macaroni. I mean, really, this thing is awful. And my dad acted like he was all proud of it — put it on top of the piano in the living

44

room and everything. So anyway, no macaroni projects today. And that means that since Ms. Blume is the only one with a key, she came back over the weekend and locked the closets. That's super weird, right? Especially since it looked to the teacher who went to her house like no one had been there since Thursday and she left her dog all alone. That's a good mystery. Plus, if she's supposed to be getting married this weekend right down the street, like my sister said, why would she go away before her wedding? Why can't the school find her?"

Alec Flint agreed that the whole thing was super weird.

"Listen," he said. "What if you help me with my mystery, and I'll help you with yours?" This way, he would have a partner, and two mysteries were always better than one. At least, he figured that was the case.

"You mean, like, we'd be partners?" Gina asked.

That's exactly what Alec Flint meant.

"Totally," he said. "Like Toody and Muldoon."

"Who?" asked Gina.

"It's from an old TV show," said Alec. "A really funny one."

"Whatever you say, partner." Gina shrugged. "I guess I should teach you the secret code, then, so we can send each other super-sleuth messages."

Gina smiled big and wide, just like Princess Jasmine did in the movie.

"Yeah," said Alec, a little worried he wouldn't be good at learning the code, having never learned one before. "So . . . what's a Zoovitz?"

"Not Zoovitz," Gina said. "*Zoovtiz*. It's my sister's name in code. Here, I'll show you the code and you figure out my sister's name."

Gina took a piece of paper and wrote carefully in all capital letters:

A B C D E F G H I J K L M N O P Q R S T U V W X Y Z
Z Y X W V U T S R Q P O N M L K J I H G F E D C B A

"See," she said, "whenever you want to write a word, you spell it with the letters underneath the letters you really want to use. So 'hello' in secret code is 'svool.'"

"Oh, I see," said Alec Flint. "So your sister's name is . . ."

Alec took a minute to write things down on his paper.

". . . Allegra! Your sister's name is Allegra."

"You got it," said Gina. "And the best part is when you memorize which letters are which, so you don't need the cheat sheet anymore. But that comes with practice."

"Cool," said Alec, thinking he knew the perfect way to practice. "I'm going to write you a whole note in code. And I'll try to memorize the letters."

It took Alec Flint most of the class to write. The letters were hard to memorize, but he kept plugging along. When he was finished, the note said:

Trmz,

Gsv gsrmt zylfg gsv nfhvfn rh gsrh: r hzd lmv lu gsv hvxfirgb tfziwh drgs hlnvgsrmt rm srh klxpvg gszg ollpvw orpv z tlow xlrm. Zmw tlow xlrmh dviv lmv lu gsv gsrmth nrhhrmt uiln gsv hglovm vesryrg. Hl r gsrmp Uvimzmwl gsv tfziw nrtsg yv gsv gsrvu. Xzm blf gsrmp lu z dzb dv xzm tvg rmgl gsv nfhvfn gl hovfgs?

— Zovx*

Gina quickly decoded the letter and wrote one back to Alec. It said:

Zovx,

Nzbyv dv xlfow qfhg zhp lmv lu lfi kzivmgh gl gzpv fh gl gsv nfhvfn — dv xlfow hzb rg'h uli z hxsllo kilqvxg li hlnvgsrmt. Nzbyv dv xlfow wl gszg glnliild? Xzm blf nvvg nv rm gsv zig illn zugvi hxsllo glwzb? R yvg gsviv ziv xofvh sviv uli gsv Nh. Yofnv nbhgvib.

— Trmz*

Alec took a little longer to decode Gina's letter than she had taken to decode the one he had written. Gina didn't even have to look at the code

49

key at all. He was a little annoyed that she wanted to solve her own mystery before his, but figured it sounded like the easier mystery anyway, and that it would be good to get that one out of the way. Then Alec thought about his bus and what his father would do if he missed it. He wrote back to Gina.

R dlfow, yfg R'w nrhh gsv yfh.*

Gina quickly read the note and wrote back:

Nb nln droo gzpv blf slnv. Wvzo?*

Alec Flint decoded her note and wrote back one word to Gina, his new honest-to-goodness detective partner:

Bvh.*

* See page 176 for code translation

Chapter 4

Tater Tots Do Not Go with Pizza

When Alec Flint got back to his classroom, he looked up at the schedule on the bulletin board. It was time for social studies. Alec groaned. He had learned very quickly that social studies in the month of October meant one thing: Christopher Columbus.

Just as Alec Flint feared, when Mrs. Jones clapped her hands for everyone's attention, she said that they would be learning more about Christopher Columbus's voyages to America. The minute she said that, Gina started scribbling a note in code. It said:

Zovx,

Kzb zggvmgrlm! Gsrh nrtsg yv svokufo uli lfi xzhv.

— Trmz*

After he decoded the note, Alec rolled his eyes a little and then formed the words, "You got it," with his mouth. Gina smiled. Alec paid attention. Though now he wasn't quite sure if he had made the right decision about a detective partner. Gina was a little bossy.

Mrs. Jones started talking again. "Does anyone know why Christopher Columbus set off from Spain in the first place?" she asked the class.

A few people raised their hands. One of those hands belonged to Alec Flint. Another belonged to Gina. The third belonged to a boy on the other side of the room named Roy Michaels, who Alec usually played soccer with at lunchtime. And the last one belonged to Emily Berg.

Mrs. Jones called on Emily.

* See page 176 for code translation

"He left Spain to come to America because people wouldn't let him go to the church he wanted for Christmas," Emily said.

Emily Berg was wrong. Alec scrunched down in his seat and felt embarrassed for her. Then he whispered to Gina, "I think she got him confused with the Pilgrims and Thanksgiving."

Gina shook her head at Emily, who didn't know the *Mayflower* from the *Santa María*.

"Well, that's not quite correct. . . ." Mrs. Jones said. "Does anyone have anything else to add? Roy?"

"He was looking for a trade route to Japan and China, even

though he called it the Indies," Roy Michaels said. "He wanted to be able to trade stuff they had in Europe for silk and spices and gold."

"Good!" said Mrs. Jones. "That's right."

Roy was smart. And his best subject was social studies. He liked to read history books for fun — the nonfiction kind. Alec would've given the same answer, except he didn't know about trading for gold. He thought Columbus already had gold. But why did he think that? Alec Flint put his hand down and rubbed his hair, trying to remember. Gina was still waving her hand in the air.

"Yes, Gina?" Mrs. Jones asked.

"And that's why he called the Native Americans 'Indians.' When he hit land, he thought it was the Indies," she said, "even though it was really the Bahamas."

"Yes!" said Mrs. Jones. "Now, does anyone know what Columbus brought with him on the *Niña*?"

Alec Flint tentatively raised his hand. It seemed like the right thought got rubbed into his brain.

Alec remembered seeing the pile of gold coins in the museum the day before. The coins he thought were worth either three thousand or a million dollars. The coins that were the reason he decided he had to be a super sleuth about the missing exhibit in the first place, because maybe there was one in Fernando-call-me-Frank's pocket. It didn't make much sense for Columbus to bring gold if he was looking to trade for gold, but . . .

"Yes, Alec?" Mrs. Jones asked. "Do you know?"

Alec closed his eyes and pictured the exhibit hall and the plaque next to the glass box holding the coins, just like he had when he walked through the empty exhibit before school. He wanted to double-check. Alec could remember better when he closed his eyes. And this time his memory told him he was right.

"Gold coins," he said. "Lots of them."

"Well, not quite," said Mrs. Jones. "Columbus was *looking* for gold. What he brought with him — ready for this, class? — was animals! He brought cows and pigs and chickens on the *Niña* to feed his crew. Isn't that funny?"

Alec Flint's eyes snapped open. He was sure there was a pile of gold coins at the museum exhibit and that the plaque said it was something Columbus was going to trade. And that he brought it on the *Niña*. One hundred percent sure.

"So they didn't have gold coins at all?" Alec asked his teacher.

"Probably not," said Mrs. Jones. "The sailors were not usually rich men. Columbus may have had a gold ring or something given to him by the king and queen, but not gold coins."

"Oh," Alec said, no longer paying attention to Mrs. Jones.

He quickly pulled a fresh piece of paper out of his binder and wrote to Gina:

R pmld gsviv dviv tlow xlrmh rm gsv vesryrg gszg tlg hglovm. Dv szev gl tvg yzxp gl gsv nfhvfn.*

* See page 176 for code translation

She quickly read the note and wrote back to him:

Glnliíld. Wlm'g dlhhb.*

After doing a whole bunch of Christopher Columbus worksheets about geography and where America was in relation to where Europe and Asia were on the globe, Alec Flint felt his stomach grumble.

Gina must've heard the grumble because she giggled and wrote in code:

Sfmtib?*

Alec Flint was embarrassed. But he was also lucky because, according to the schedule on the bulletin board, it was time for lunch.

Alec waited on the hot-lunch line with Roy in front of him and Gina behind him. The three of them were in line on a good day, a very good day — the hot lunch at Laurel Hollows East was

* See page 177 for code translation

pizza. For some reason that Alec Flint couldn't figure out, pizza was always served with Tater Tots and chocolate pudding. He could understand the chocolate pudding, but what was the story with the Tater Tots? Tater Tots totally did not go with pizza. As far as Alec Flint was concerned, Tater Tots went with burgers or steak. And maybe — just maybe — with chicken fingers.

Of course, that didn't mean Alec threw the Tater Tots away on pizza days. Quite the contrary — he ate them before he even took a bite of the pizza. But mostly that was so he wouldn't burn the roof of his mouth. Alec Flint hated how when he burned the roof of his mouth, the mouth skin would blister and then peel off, but not all the way, and then he'd have this piece of skin hanging in his mouth, dangling to where he could wobble it with his tongue. Ew. He hated that even more than he hated Christopher Columbus.

Apparently, Gina was curious about the Tater Tots too.

"Hey, Alec," Gina said to the back of Alec's head as they moved along the line, scooting their lunch trays from the pizza lady to the Tater Tot lady.

Alec turned around.

"Why don't they give us something that goes with pizza, like garlic knots or garlic bread?" she asked.

Alec shrugged. "Dunno," he said.

"At my uncle's pizza place he doesn't even have Tater Tots . . . or chocolate pudding," Gina said as the pudding lady glumped a blob of pudding in one of her tray compartments. "He has Italian ices for dessert there and *zeppole*. No pudding."

"What's a *zeppole*?" Alec Flint asked.

"Dough that's fried and then sprinkled with lots of powdered sugar. One day you should come to my uncle's restaurant and I'll make you one for free."

"Okay," Alec Flint said. Gina was the only kid Alec had ever been around who made him feel like he wasn't very smart. She could write in code, and make desserts named *zeppole*, and she could even solve Math Madness in the Do Now. Every time. With more than one solution.

As Alec was thinking about this, he felt someone poke his shoulder.

"Hey, Flint." It was Roy Michaels. "You in for soccer today?"

"I don't think so today," Alec said. "Count me out."

Alec Flint had some serious thinking to do and needed recess to mull things over. He had to think about his plan for solving the mystery of the Christopher Columbus exhibit. And also maybe he should spend some time thinking about Gina's mystery of the missing Ms. Blume. He wanted to prove to Gina that he was smart too. Or, maybe more than Gina, he wanted to prove it to himself. He had to show that he could be a sleuth for real.

After Alec got his little carton of milk — school lunches always came with milk, either chocolate or regular (Alec preferred regular) — he paid with two singles and two quarters and went to his normal table, where he sat with Roy and four other soccer guys: Joe, Andy, Carlos, and L.J. They all called Alec "Flint." He called them Joe, Andy, Carlos, and L.J.

When Alec turned his head after he sat down, he saw Gina look at him for a long while and then turn and sit at Emily and Carrie's table. He didn't even know she was friends with them.

Oops! Too late Alec realized that Gina had wanted to sit with him at lunch. Maybe to talk about their plan for later in the art room. Or their plan for the next day at the museum. Oh well. He figured they could talk during recess.

But during recess, Gina was doing the monkey bars with Emily and Carrie and two other girls who Alec Flint sometimes got confused. Their names were Sarah and Stacey, but he could never remember which one was Sarah and which one was Stacey. They both had wavy brown hair and hadn't been in Alec's class in first, second, or third grade. In fact, they weren't in his class this year either. But they had been in some class for some grade with Emily and Carrie, because all

four of those girls hung out together during recess every day. And now it looked like Gina hung out with them too. How annoying when he needed to talk to her.

Alec Flint sat on the bench in the playground near the monkey bars and rubbed ideas into his brain. The first idea had to do with the gold in the exhibit. Maybe Mrs. Jones was wrong about what Columbus brought on his voyage and what he was looking for in the Indies. Teachers weren't usually wrong about things, but it was possible. He would maybe have to check on that in the library or in his social studies textbook. Or on his computer if he could get the right Web site. King Ferdinand and Queen Isabella could've given Columbus gold coins to trade. They might've had a whole lot of them. Plus, the anonymous benefactor said it was true, and rich guys didn't lie. Or did they? Alec wasn't sure. Maybe they did.

As Alec was thinking, he was also sort of watching the girls on the monkey bars. Gina was really good at getting across to the other side. Alec Flint was not surprised. Gina went fast. After a few tries she even swung herself forward so far that she could skip over every other bar and go faster still. Stacey and Sarah (or Sarah and Stacey) both had the same monkey-bar style. They went slowly and carefully but got across every time. Carrie sometimes swung too far or not far enough. When that happened, she missed the bar and ended up hanging by one hand. Then she had to jump off. Emily was a whole other story. Emily couldn't always get to the first bar. In fact, most of the time she didn't.

Alec Flint watched Gina jump up and forward and grab the first bar. Then he watched Sarah and Stacey and Carrie jump up and forward and grab the first bar. Then he watched Emily jump up. And miss the first bar. She did it again and again and kept landing on her sneakers on the ground. Then she tried one more time and fell. She left the monkey bars and came to sit next to Alec on the bench so she could inspect her legs.

"Hey, Alec," she said, not very bouncily, as she rolled up her pants. Her knees were scraped a little but not so bad.

"The nurse'll give you a Band-Aid, if you go," said Alec Flint.

"Yeah," said Emily. "Whatever. I'm not even bleeding."

Then everything was quiet between Alec and Emily for a little while, until Emily said, "Why can't I do it, Alec? Why can't I get onto the monkey bars like everyone else?"

Alec looked at Emily differently than he usually did.

"For real?" he said. "You wanna know?"

Emily nodded.

"It's because you're only jumping up and not forward," he said. Then he got off the bench to demonstrate. He jumped up and landed in the same spot. Then he jumped up and forward and landed a good six inches in front of where he started.

"See?" he asked Emily Berg. "If you jump up and forward at the same time, you'll be able to grab the bar."

Emily was back to her old bouncy self.

"Wow!" she said. "Thanks!"

Then Emily ran back over to the monkey bars and jumped up and forward and grabbed the first one. She slowly but surely swung herself to the end, where she turned and gave Alec a big smile. He turned pink, right to the tips of his ears. But it made him feel good that he'd done a nice job observing Emily and figuring things out.

Alec looked at his detective watch. It was almost time for the recess bell. Might as well be early. He got up and started walking out of the playground to where the classes had to line up so their teachers could pick them up after lunch. Before he got out of the playground area, he felt a poke in his back and turned around. It was

Gina. She handed him a note scrawled on a napkin. Alec realized that this was his second napkin note of the day — first his dad's and now Gina's. Maybe the people he knew should start carrying around paper.

He unfolded Gina's napkin note, and it said:

R szev z kozm lm sld gl tvg rmgl gsv zig illn. Nvvg nv gsviv urev nrmfgvh zugvi gsv wrhnrhhzo yvoo.

— Trmz

K.H. R ulitrev blf uli mlg hrggrmt drgs nv zg ofmxs.*

Alec was getting so fast at the code that he knew in his head which letters stood for what, and while he was waiting for Mrs. Jones to pick up the class, he pulled out his pen and wrote them into the note so he could figure out what it said. Alec Flint was glad that Gina wasn't mad at him, but sheesh, he wasn't planning on eating lunch with her every day! What about the soccer guys?

* See page 177 for code translation

Chapter 5

Shiny and Also Furry

In the afternoon, Alec's class had SSR — Sustained Silent Reading — which really just meant reading quietly to yourself until Mrs. Jones said to stop and, after that, language arts, where the class broke into groups, each group reading a different book. Gina and Roy were in Alec's group, along with two other kids — Mala Sharma and Jonathan Shin. They were all reading *Prairie Songs,* which Gina said was one of her favorite books of all time — she'd read it in third grade too — but Alec and Roy thought it could use some more fighting and fewer girl things like moms and babies and crying.

During language arts, Alec wondered how Gina thought she could get them inside the art room if the door was locked. Did she know how to pick locks? That would just be too much for Alec Flint. He made a note in his head that he had to learn how to pick locks. And fast. It really was something every sleuth should know, in case there was a search warrant and an uncooperative witness who wouldn't let you inside.

When language arts was over, Mrs. Jones clapped her hands and said that everyone should get their jackets and bags. "Don't forget to pack your homework folders," she said.

Alec Flint did not forget to pack his homework folder. He zipped his backpack and was the first one in line for dismissal. He remembered just then that he didn't have a note saying he wasn't going on the bus. But maybe since he hadn't gone on the bus in the morning it wouldn't be a problem? *Hmm.* Maybe he should just —

"Mrs. Jones?" Gina said, popping up next to Alec. "Alec Flint is coming home with me today. He doesn't have a note, but you can even ask my mom. She's waiting by the Willow Street door. Is that okay?"

"Is that true, Alec?" Mrs. Jones asked.

"Mm-hmm." Alec nodded, picking up Gina's story. "It's 'cause my dad has to work late on a case and my mom is away for business. She went to Texas again."

"All right," said Mrs. Jones. "Normally I'd follow up on this story, but you two are good kids and I have an appointment after school today. Alec, I'll tell your bus not to wait for you."

"Thanks, Mrs. Jones," Alec and Gina said at the same time.

"Jinx!" Gina said to Alec. "Now you can't talk till I say your whole name."

"That's dumb," said Alec. "I'm talking."

Gina shrugged. "Whatever. Now you've got bad luck for a whole year."

Alec wanted to make her take that back. He was *not* having bad luck for a year because of her dumb jinx, but there were more important things to do, so he just rolled his eyes up toward his brain and said, "Whatever you say."

The dismissal bell rang at 2:42. A palindrome. Palindromes were always lucky. Alec's mom's name was a palindrome — Hannah. Same forward as it was backward.

Gina looked at Alec. "Let's go!" she said. And the two of them walked as quickly as they could to the art room — running was not allowed in the halls of East, and neither of them wanted to get detention.

When they got into the art room hall, Gina jogged a little ahead of Alec. It wasn't exactly running, but it was close. She called out something Alec couldn't understand and the custodian who was walking in front of them stopped and turned around. Then she said some more things to the custodian. Alec Flint realized that Gina was not talking in English. *Good grief,* thought Alec.

The conversation ended with the custodian taking a key ring off of his belt and unlocking the art room door. Then he walked away. Gina yelled after him, "*Grazie!*" To Alec Flint it sounded like "grat-see-yay."

"What," asked Alec Flint, "was that all about? What did you say to him? What language was that?"

"The last thing was 'thank you,'" said Gina. "It turns out that he speaks Italian, like my family. I met him two days ago when I left my math book in the classroom and tried to find someone who could unlock the door on a Saturday. Just now I told him I forgot my favorite eraser in the art room and wanted to look for it. He said he was happy to help. Mostly, I think,

because I asked in Italian. He must think I'm so forgetful . . . first the math book, now the eraser." Gina laughed.

Alec Flint couldn't believe that Gina could speak a language that wasn't English.

"Where did you learn Italian?" he demanded. "When?"

"My family just speaks it," she said. "Like, in the house, the way your family probably speaks English. I learned it my whole life. Come *on*! We have to check out the art room."

"Yeah," said Alec Flint, following her, and all of a sudden thinking about how his dad was going to try to come home early so there would be no Mrs. McGrady. "And we've gotta do it fast because my dad is probably waiting at home for me to get off the bus."

There was a marshmallowy feeling in Alec's stomach. He hated lying. Especially when he could get caught. By his dad. Alec gulped hard and walked into the art room with Gina.

Alec and Gina started with the closets. They pulled the doorknobs and pried at the cracks around the edges, but the doors stayed shut. It was just like doing a police search, but a little bit illegal because they didn't have a warrant that gave them permission. Still, Alec was sure that sometimes super sleuths had to do things without permission.

"Why do you think she locked the doors anyway?" Alec Flint asked Gina.

"Dunno." Gina shrugged. "Maybe she bought some expensive jewelry or art or something and was afraid it would get stolen at her house, so she locked it in here. Or maybe . . . I don't know any other maybes."

"Maybe she's a criminal!" said Alec Flint. "Maybe she killed someone! And the body's in there! And she had to run away!"

Gina rolled her eyes at Alec.

"She did not kill anybody, Alec Flint," Gina

said. "Ms. Blume is an art teacher. Art teachers don't kill people. They just teach art."

Alec Flint shrugged. He knew from his dad that sometimes the people you least expected could be criminals. Like when they found out the guy who carried groceries to your car at the Food, Glorious Food grocery store was stealing people's wallets. An art teacher could definitely be a criminal. A killer, even. Alec peeked through a crack in the closet door, but it was too dark in there to see anything. When he turned around to look for Gina, she was already on the other side of the room.

"Come *on!*" she said. "Help me check the teacher's desk for keys. Ms. Levine might have missed them. Maybe they were here all along and a custodian or someone locked the closets by accident over the weekend. Maybe Ms. Blume didn't take the keys home with her or whatever."

Alec went over and opened one of the drawers of Ms. Blume's desk. He didn't find any keys in there, but after only a couple of minutes of searching, Alec found something he knew was a clue. He started slowly rubbing his hair.

"Gina," he said softly. Then louder, "Gina! Look at this."

Gina looked.

"So?" she asked. "It's a framed newspaper article with a picture in it."

"Do you know who that man is in the picture?" Alec Flint asked back.

Gina shook her head no.

"It's the curator of the museum. The one who got the secret rich guy to donate all the stuff for the Columbus exhibit."

Smiling up at Alec in black and white was the face of that weirdo Dr. Glumsfeld. He was holding Ms. Blume's hand.

"It looks like they're in love," said Gina.

"Ew," said Alec Flint.

Then Gina took the picture frame from Alec and read the newspaper article. It said that Ms. Blume and Dr. Glumsfeld were engaged to be married. And the wedding was this coming Saturday at the church down the street. Just like Allegra had said.

"Nice find," Gina said to Alec.

"Yeah," said Alec, "I bet Dr. Glumsfeld knows where Ms. Blume is."

"Definitely," said Gina. "When we go to the museum, maybe we can ask him! That is, if we see him."

"He doesn't like kids so much," Alec told her.

"We'll figure something out. . . . Here," Gina said, holding out her backpack. "We can put all the clues in my bag to look at later."

"Umm," said Alec. "I don't know if we should do that. It's kind of like stealing."

Gina's eyebrows scrunched together. "But if we don't take it, it might disappear, and it's our best clue so far. We can put it back after we find Ms. Blume."

Alec saw her point.

"Okay," he said. "As long as we put it back later."

"Definitely," said Gina.

Alec was on a roll, because right after he found the picture, he found a flashlight. And that flashlight gave him a great super-sleuth idea.

"Come *on*," he said to Gina, just the way she'd

said it to him before. He walked back to the closet and shined the flashlight into the crack in the door he'd noticed earlier. Whatever was inside reflected the flashlight's beam. It was shiny. And also furry.

"Well," Alec said to Gina, "it's not a dead body or art or jewelry. But I don't know what it is."

Gina looked too. "Me neither. It's a furry-shiny something. Or maybe two things? One that's furry and the other that's shiny? Maybe it's art supplies."

"Dead end," said Alec Flint. "Let's see if there are any other clues."

Gina found one. Crumpled in a ball next to the garbage pail, it was a page from Ms. Blume's day planner with last Thursday's date on top. The day she disappeared. Ms. Blume had written:

4:00 – meet TG in office

Alec and Gina weren't sure what it meant, but they knew it meant *something,* so they added it to the newspaper article already in Gina's backpack and then quickly walked out of the art room, shutting the door behind them. It was getting late, and Gina's mom was waiting.

"I think I like being a detective," Gina said as she zipped her backpack.

"Yeah," Alec said. "Me too."

But even though he liked being a detective, Alec Flint was not happy. He was no closer to solving either one of his cases.

"*Ciao!*" Gina yelled to the custodian as they walked by him.

Chow? What did that mean? Maybe Gina would make Alec a dictionary and teach him Italian too. Since they were partners and all.

By the time Alec and Gina got to Mrs. Rossi's car, the marshmallowy feeling had come back. Only now it felt like a whole bag of marshmallows that were melty and gooey. He hoped the bus hadn't passed by his house yet. He hoped his dad wasn't worried.

Alec looked up at Mrs. Rossi — her car was big and high. A Jeep Liberty Sport: dark green. Alec Flint liked Jeep Liberty Sports and loved green. Inside the car Mrs. Rossi was writing something down on a pad of paper leaned against the steering wheel. In the backseat, strapped in, sat a smaller version of Gina with

the same long black hair and brown eyes. Alec knew that it had to be her sister, Allegra. The one who made the ugly noodle project on Friday. The one who knew the secret code. Allegra was reading a book.

"Hi, Mom," Gina said. "This is Alec Flint. We're working on a sort of project together, so we had to stay a little late to plan things out. Can we take him home? I mean, to his home, not ours. He missed the bus."

Mrs. Rossi looked up. "Hi, Gigi," she said. "Hi, Alec, nice to meet you — no problem taking you home. You know, I've interviewed your father before for an article or two in the *Laurel Hollows Herald*. In fact, I'm scheduled to talk to him tomorrow about this Christopher Columbus exhibit theft. Sounds like it's got the police stumped."

Alec gave Gina a serious look. It meant: We have to help my dad and solve that case. It also meant: Let's keep this sleuthing thing secret. Gina nodded. She understood.

Then the two of them climbed into the Jeep. Mrs. Rossi put the pad that she was writing on down next to her in the front of the car. Alec tried to see what it said, but the words were really small and Alec couldn't read them from the backseat.

"Thank you, Mrs. Rossi," Alec Flint said, remembering his manners. "My house is Forty-two Oak Park Road. It's near the duck pond."

"No problem," said Mrs. Rossi. "And please, call me Francesca. When I hear someone say Mrs. Rossi, I think of Gina and Allegra's grandmother."

"It's silly that you say that, Mom," Allegra said, still looking at the book in her lap. "There are lots of Mrs. Rossis. You're Mrs. Rossi, and Nonna's Mrs. Rossi, and Zia Teri is Mrs. Rossi too, because she married Zio Nick. And if Zio Carmine gets married, that *zia* will be another Mrs. Rossi. It shouldn't just make you think of Nonna."

Gina rolled her eyes at Alec. "It doesn't matter, Allegra," she said. "Mom likes being called Francesca, okay?"

"I'm just saying," muttered Allegra. But it seemed that she'd already lost interest in the conversation and was back to reading her book.

Alec was still stuck on the *zio* and *zia* business. He figured out that Nonna was Gina's grandmother . . . and thought that *zio* and *zia* meant "uncle" and "aunt." At least, that would make sense because of the same-last-name stuff. Maybe Gina really could teach him Italian and then he could call his grandma something other than just "Grandma."

"Thanks, Gigi," Mrs. Rossi (Francesca, not the Nonna or any of the Zias) said. "It's nice having my defense attorney around."

Gina laughed. "My mom thinks I should be a lawyer when I grow up," she told Alec. "I think that might be cool, but what I really want to do is be the president — the first girl ever who's president."

"Rock on, Gi," Mrs. Rossi said.

Alec realized very quickly that Mrs. Rossi was a different kind of mom than his mom was. And different from his dad too. She seemed almost like a kid, but a grown-up kid. It was kind of cool. But he wondered if she'd be good at taking care of people when they had the chicken pox, or putting Band-Aids on knee scrapes.

"Forty-two Oak Park Road!" said Mrs. Rossi, pulling into Alec's driveway. "Here we are."

"Thanks," Alec said, getting out of the car and pulling his backpack along after him.

"What's your phone number?" Gina said, before Alec closed the door. "In case we need to work on our project later."

Alec gave Gina his phone number. The only girl who ever called him — not counting family members — was Emily Berg, when she spilled milk on her homework folder. Or let her baby brother chew on her homework folder. Or forgot her homework folder altogether. But mostly, if

Emily wanted to tell him something, she just knocked on his door, being his next-door neighbor and all.

Mrs. Rossi watched Alec walk to his front door. And turn the knob. It was locked. Alec did not have a key. His parents said nine wasn't old enough for a key. Then, too late, he remembered that if his dad wasn't home he was supposed to go to Mrs. McGrady's house. Which he did not want to do. Out of the corner of his eye, he saw Emily, her brother, Benny, and their mom playing on the lawn next door.

"Mrs. — umm, Francesca," he said to Gina's mom. "It looks like my dad's not home yet, so I'll just stay at the Bergs' until he gets here." Alec had done that before, and none of the Bergs seemed to have minded. Neither had his father.

Mrs. Rossi backed the car out of the driveway and a little bit down the street until she was in front of the Bergs' house.

"Hey!" she yelled out the window. "Is it okay

if I leave this guy with you until his dad gets home?"

Mrs. Berg looked up. "Oh, sure," she said. "Alec's an old pal."

Alec walked over to Emily's yard and dropped his bag on the grass. Mrs. Rossi zoomed off. Alec Flint was relieved in his brain. An afternoon with the Bergs was *much* better than an afternoon with Mrs. McGrady.

Chapter 6

Dancing the Part of a Tree

Hey, Alec Flint?" Emily said, looking up from some tickle game she was playing with Benny. "Hey, Alec?"

Alec noticed that everything Emily said sounded like a question, even if it wasn't.

"Yeah?" said Alec, experimenting with talking like Emily.

"Do you want to come to my dance show?"

Her dance show? Emily Berg was in a dance show? She could barely run in P.E. without tripping over her feet.

"Ummm," said Alec Flint, not really wanting to go to her dance show at all and thinking super fast about how to get out of it. "When is it?"

"This weekend. It's in the school auditorium," Emily answered. "We're doing the *Cinderella* ballet — well, a kid version of it."

"Oh," said Alec. The Cinderella part wasn't half bad — the ugly stepsisters were kind of funny — but the ballet part? Nuh-uh. No way was Alec Flint going to watch Emily Berg in a ballet. In fact, no way was he going to watch a ballet, period. "I think I might be busy this weekend. My mom is coming home from her trip on Friday. So, you know."

Emily nodded as if she did know.

"But, umm," said Alec Flint, "why don't you tell me about the ballet? Are you Cinderella or something?"

Emily looked a little sad. "I *wish* I was Cinderella. I tried out for her, but I got the part of a tree."

"A tree?" asked Alec Flint. "I didn't know there were any trees in *Cinderella*."

"There are in this one," Emily told him. "I have to sway happily when the prince finds Cinderella."

"Oh," said Alec. "That's an important part."

"You think so?" said Emily.

"Totally," said Alec. The truth was he wasn't so sure if it was an important part. In fact, he thought it probably wasn't, but he didn't want Emily to feel bad that she wasn't Cinderella. And then Alec had an inspiration about Gina's case.

"Where do you practice for the ballet show?" he asked Emily, figuring they would practice where they performed.

"At school. On the weekends. It's kind of cool to be there with no other kids."

Just what Alec thought.

"Hey, Emily," he said. "Any chance you saw any teachers this past weekend?"

Emily tilted her head to one side. "No teachers," she said. "But there was this one weird man who was there yesterday — not a teacher but a grown-up. I was practicing my happy swaying in the hallway where the art room is, and I saw an adult there, so I went back to the practice area because of the rule of no being alone with strangers."

This is exactly the kind of thing Alec was hoping Emily would remember. He thought it would be Ms. Blume, but this guy — whoever he was — could've had something to do with Ms. Blume. Maybe Emily wouldn't be such a bad sleuth after all.

"Do you remember anything about him?" he asked.

"Not really," said Emily. "Just that his walking was really quiet. I couldn't really see him because he was all the way at the other end of the hallway, and most of the lights were off."

Quiet walking? Alec knew two people who

walked especially quietly: Fernando-call-me-Frank and Dr. Glumsfeld.

"And when he saw me?" Emily continued. "He whispered really loudly from down the hall. 'Well, if it isn't a young female Homo sapiens, swaying to and fro!' It was super strange. I didn't even know what it meant. Why do you care about weird grown-ups in the hallways anyway, Alec Flint? And how did you know to ask about that?"

"No special reason," said Alec, secretly rubbing thoughts into the back of his brain. The part right near his sweatshirt hood. "Just curious."

Now he was thinking that the guy Emily described was maybe Dr. Glumsfeld because of the quiet walking plus big words. That would make a little sense since he and Ms. Blume were getting married. So he could've had the keys from her. But what would he have locked in the closets? And where was Ms. Blume? Why wasn't she with him at the school? Could she be staying at

Dr. Glumsfeld's house? But then why leave her dog? And why not pick up the mail?

Thoughts swirled around in Alec's brain like a milk shake in a blender — could his case and Gina's case be linked? Could Ms. Blume be the anonymous donor? Alec figured he'd have to think about all this a little more before he could talk to Gina. Or even before he could ask Emily if she thought the guy might be Glumsfeld, since she'd met him and all. He didn't want to say Ms. Blume was *anything,* without any evidence. That was not allowed. Alec knew that from his dad. You always needed evidence — just thinking things didn't matter without proof.

"Hey, want to play hopscotch?" Emily asked.

But just then an unmarked vehicle drove into Alec's driveway, and Officer Flint stepped out. "Alexander Edward Flint," he boomed across the lawn. "Did you not go to Mrs. McGrady's like I told you to?"

Alec wasn't too worried about his dad being

really mad, since he'd done this before and never gotten in much trouble. His dad knew how much he hated going to Mrs. McGrady's.

"Guilty as charged, Dad," he said.

"Thank you, Alyssa," Officer Flint said to Mrs. Berg. And then, "Alec, home!"

Alec waved good-bye to Emily, picked up his backpack, and walked across the lawn to his house. And his dad. Who had a big box of pizza.

The Flint men went inside and ate dinner. While they were eating, Alec remembered that marshmallowy feeling in his stomach. In fact, it was coming back.

"Uh, Dad," Alec said, midchew. "I have to tell you something."

Officer Flint peered at Alec. "Okay," he said. "Shoot."

Alec chewed his pizza twice. "I didn't go home on the bus today. I went with Gina's mom, Francesca Rossi. She drove me here."

Alec Flint hadn't planned on telling in advance. It just seemed like something that he had to do. And the minute he told, the marshmallowy feeling went away.

Officer Flint looked long and hard at Alec. "Listen, Al," he said. "I'm sure there's a very good reason why you didn't take the bus home, and why you didn't go to Mrs. McGrady's like I asked, but right now I'm having trouble solving the Christopher Columbus case at the museum, and I don't really want to deal with this. Okay?"

Alec gulped the mainly unchewed pizza in his mouth. And as he did, he remembered he had pizza for lunch that day. Oh well, not like it bothered him. He loved pizza. Then he started to feel the unchewed pizza glump getting stuck in his throat and had to grab for his water.

"Okay, Dad," he said when the glump got unstuck. "I just wanted to tell you." Alec was also thinking about telling his dad about the coin shape he thought he saw in Fernando the security guard's pocket, but then remembered the rule about having real evidence before you said something bad about someone.

"Sure, Al," said Officer Flint. Then he sighed. "Hey, why don't you go work on that Columbus report you were telling me about?"

"All right," Alec said, and went to the computer room, dropping his cup and plate in the kitchen sink on the way there.

The thing that Alec knew after nine years of living with Officer Flint was that when he was having trouble with a case, he was not fun to be around. He was cranky, like Emily's brother, Benny, when he didn't take a nap. And he didn't so much want to talk to anyone. Including Alec.

Alec pulled out his detective notebook and looked at the part that was sometimes an assignment pad. Written there from that morning were his notes to himself about doing the Christopher

Columbus paper. In the detective part there was a note about Fernando maybe having a gold coin in his pocket. And one about finding out if Mrs. Jones was right about the gold coins. So Alec pulled out his social studies spiral notebook — green, wide-ruled — and went to one of the information Web sites Mrs. Jones had made them write down last week in class. There didn't seem to be anything about gold or what Columbus brought on the *Niña,* so Alec started writing stuff down for the report. He was making lists, copying information neatly off of the computer screen in front of him.

"Things That Were Not in America before Christopher Columbus Got Here," Alec Flint wrote. Then he listed: *"1) People who were not Native Americans, 2) A disease named smallpox, 3) Spaghetti."* Alec realized he would need more things on that list if he was going to use it for his report, and he couldn't find anything else on the Web site to add. So he started a new list.

"*Things That Were Not in the World at All When Christopher Columbus Was Around,*" he wrote. Then he read through the information on the screen and listed: "*1) Plastic, 2) The word America, 3) Computers, 4) Telephones, 5) TV, 6) Cars, 7) Airplanes.*" Alec stopped taking notes and thought how different his life would have been if he were a sailor in 1492. He wouldn't have been able to watch cartoons on Saturday mornings or push the button that made the top open on his mom's convertible. He wouldn't have been able to fly on an airplane to see his cousins.

Alec shook his head at the thought of those poor sailors with no cartoons, then kept going on his list: "*8) Video games, 9) Markers, 10) Cap'n Crunch cereal, 11) Fruit snacks.*" Alec had stopped looking at the computer screen. In fact, items 8, 9, 10, and 11 he had made up himself, but he was pretty sure he was right because of number 1, no plastic. Video games were made of plastic and so were the outside part of markers.

Cap'n Crunch and fruit snacks were wrapped in plastic. No plastic—no video games or markers. No Cap'n Crunch or fruit snacks. No a lot of things, actually.

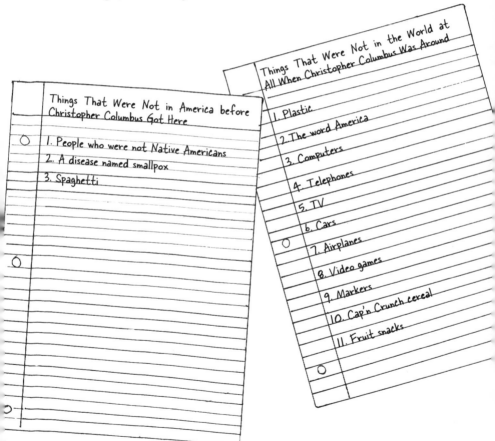

Things That Were Not in America before Christopher Columbus Got Here

1. People who were not Native Americans
2. A disease named smallpox
3. Spaghetti

Things That Were Not in the World at All When Christopher Columbus Was Around

1. Plastic
2. The word America
3. Computers
4. Telephones
5. TV
6. Cars
7. Airplanes
8. Video games
9. Markers
10. Cap'n Crunch cereal
11. Fruit snacks

Alec Flint decided what his report would be about — the way that Christopher Columbus's life would have been different if plastic had been invented in 1492. For example, he would have been able to wear a poncho and rain boots to stay dry when there were storms on the ocean. And he would have been able to write with a pen instead of a feather or stick or something dipped in ink. Those were good ideas. Alec wrote them down.

But before he could really get started on his report, the phone rang. Alec picked it up, noticing that it was plastic. Everything was plastic!

"Flint residence, Alec speaking," Alec said, the way his parents had taught him.

"I'm returning the phone call of one Officer Flint," said the voice on the other end.

Alec thought he recognized the voice, but he wasn't quite sure.

"Hold on one moment, please," Alec said politely.

Then he yelled through the house, "Daaaaad! Phoooone!" He was going to add, "I think it's that weird museum guy," but realized that the weird museum guy would hear him if he yelled that.

Alec listened on the phone until he heard his father pick up on another extension.

"This is Officer Flint," Alec's father said.

"This is Dr. Glumsfeld." Alec was right. It *was* the weird museum guy. Alec hung up the phone. Too late, he remembered that he could've asked him about Ms. Blume.

A little while later, Alec Flint walked into the kitchen, where his dad was sitting reading the newspaper. It was times like these, late at night, when it was just Alec and his dad in the whole big house themselves, that he missed his mom the most.

"Hey," Alec said to his dad, "what did Dr. Glumsfeld want on the phone?"

"Nothing," Alec's dad said. "He was calling me back to tell me that he won't give me the name of the anonymous donor."

"Is that important?" Alec asked.

"Yeah," said his dad. "Very important. I think the anonymous donor might have something to do with the robbery. He's the one who'll get all the insurance money if we can't find the exhibit. Glumsfeld appraised the collection at over twelve million dollars."

"Wow," said Alec Flint.

It was super strange that Dr. Glumsfeld wouldn't tell his dad the name of the anonymous donor. It made sense if the donor was a detective and needed to keep things quiet but, even so, the police got to know lots of secrets. It was part of being the police. When you asked a person a question, they had to answer it. Alec Flint wondered again if Ms. Blume was the anonymous donor and if she was a secret rich guy.

"I know," said his dad. "Listen, it looks like I'm going to be at the museum late tomorrow. Instead of Mrs. McGrady's, do you want to come there after school?"

"Yes!" said Alec, running to give his dad a hug. Going to the museum meant not getting to play outside all afternoon and staying out of the way while his dad worked, but it was *so* much better than doing nothing inside Mrs. McGrady's house that the choice was easy as pie. And then Alec Flint had a brainstorm. He'd figured out the perfect way to get Gina to the museum tomorrow too.

"Hey, Dad?" he said. "Can my new friend Gina come? Then I won't get bored."

"I don't see why not," said Officer Flint.

Alec's dad helped him find Gina's number in the phone book — Alec hadn't written down her number when she'd asked about his. Gina was excited to come along. She even said "good job" to Alec about getting them to the museum without making anyone think it was weird. Gina's mom said she would drive them after school because she had an interview with the president of the museum at four o'clock and was supposed to talk to Alec's dad right afterward. Nice.

Then Officer Flint wanted to talk to Mrs. Rossi. Alec passed him the phone. Alec Flint was not paying attention to what his dad was saying. He was deep in thought. About cases and police car partners. But when Officer Flint said the words "at the museum," Alec started to pay attention. It was too late, though, because Officer Flint started coughing and didn't say any more about the museum. In fact, he couldn't say anything at all except for, "Al, water." And even that didn't come out very clearly.

Alec ran to the cabinet where his family kept cups — he started to pull a plastic cup out of the cabinet, but decided on a fancy glass one instead.

He thought his dad might like it better, being a grown-up and all.

Alec Flint filled the glass with water from the refrigerator. Then he put it on the counter.

When Alec went to put the water pitcher back, his elbow accidentally knocked into the glass. It teetered. Alec Flint saw and tried to catch it, dropping the water pitcher in the process. But he missed. And water — a three-quarters-full pitcher of it — fell to the ground, along with the small glass, which shattered as it hit the floor.

By this time,

Officer Flint had walked over to the sink and drank from the faucet. He'd stopped coughing. He'd also gotten off the phone with Mrs. Rossi.

"Did you use a good glass, Al?" Officer Flint asked.

Alec looked at the mess at his feet.

"Yeah," he said. "I thought you'd like it better."

Officer Flint sighed. "Just stay where you are, Al. I don't want you to step on any of that shattered glass."

Alec Flint stayed where he was while his father cleaned up the water and glass. Then Officer Flint gave Alec a lesson on plastic. He took a plastic cup from the cup cabinet. He dropped it on the floor. It bounced around but didn't shatter. Plastic reminded Alec Flint of Emily Berg — the bounciness at least.

"See," Officer Flint said. "Plastic cups don't break. Glass ones do. From now on, only plastic cups. All right, Al?"

"All right," said Alec Flint.

For good measure, Officer Flint moved the glass cups to a high shelf. One that Alec could only reach with a step stool and by climbing on the counter after he stepped on the step stool.

Alec Flint felt bad about the glass. His dad didn't punish him, but Alec went into his room anyway. Alec punished himself.

Chapter 7

Basta Pizza!

The next morning Alec Flint woke up to the theme song of *Mission: Impossible*. Not because it was on TV or because someone started watching the DVD in another room or anything, but because it was programmed into his stereo as his alarm clock. In fact, it was programmed so loud that it was Officer Flint's alarm clock too. When Alec's mom was home, she left for work before *Mission: Impossible* went off, so it wasn't her alarm clock. Just the guys'.

Alec jumped out of his bed and walked across his room to turn the stereo off. The minute

111

his brain turned on, it started thinking about Ms. Blume and Dr. Glumsfeld. Ms. Blume didn't seem so much like she was rich enough to be an anonymous donor. She didn't wear fancy jewelry, and she drove an old two-toned car she called Marvin. She showed Alec's class the car through the window once. But what about those locked closets?

While Alec was getting dressed — another pair of cargo pants and a green-and-white-striped shirt — and looking for his sneakers, and brushing his teeth and gelling his hair, he kept thinking. Even while eating his Cap'n Crunch.

He was trying to come up with things that were fuzzy

and shiny. Maybe some kind of mask? Or a weird art sculpture? Alec hoped it was something that Ms. Blume made and that she wasn't a perp. Mainly because Ms. Blume was so nice. She let him paint his whole clay vase green instead of patterns because she knew how much he liked green. And once when Emily was crying because she couldn't draw a ballerina right, Ms. Blume drew it for her and even made the ballerina look like Emily. Alec really hoped Ms. Blume was not a perp. But there was still the problem of where she was. And also of Dr. Glumsfeld being at the school during the weekend. Could the cases really be connected? He'd have to discuss this possibility with Gina.

Alec Flint checked his detective watch. He had six minutes before his bus. Enough time to write a note explaining everything.

'Nlimrmt Trmz,

R gsrmp Ifi gdl xzhvh nrtsg yv xlmmvxgvw hlnvsld. Vnrob yvit hzbh hsv hzd mi. Tofnhuvow, gsv nfhvfn

113

tfb, rm gsv hxsllo szoodzb lm Hfmwzb irtsg mvzi gsv zig illn. R dlmwvi dszg rg nvzmh. Ovg'h gzop zg ofmxs.

— Zovx*

Just as Alec finished writing his note to Gina, Officer Flint came in, ready to go to work. He gave Alec two singles and two quarters for lunch, and reminded him to go with Gina to the museum, and he'd meet them at 4:30 in the empty Christopher Columbus exhibit hall.

"Hopefully I'll have this thing solved by the time you get there, Al," Officer Flint said.

"I hope so too, Dad," Alec answered. But he wasn't so sure that would happen.

Then Alec heard the bus horn honk from the street. He grabbed his backpack with one hand, his sweatshirt with the other, and raced out the door and down the driveway. He could see Emily racing down her driveway too, with Mrs. Berg following behind holding Emily's backpack and also a pink sparkly headband.

114

* See page 177 for code translation

"Emily!" Mrs. Berg was calling. "You forgot your bag! And here! Put this in your hair so it's not such a mess! Your teacher's going to think we live like animals in this house!"

But Emily was not paying attention to her mother. Alec Flint, on the other hand, had observed this situation many times and knew exactly what to do. He changed direction and ran across his front lawn, over to Mrs. Berg.

"I'll bring them to Emily," he said, grabbing the backpack and the hair thing as he ran.

"Thanks, Alec," said Mrs. Berg. "I don't know what Emily would do without you!"

Alec Flint got to the bus just in time and handed both items to Emily.

"Oh!" she said. "I didn't realize I left my bag at home! And why did you bring me a headband?"

"Your mom says your hair's a mess," Alec muttered. One problem with being a sleuth was sometimes you learned things that really weren't your business. Or at least things you didn't want to have to repeat.

"Oh," said Emily Berg. "Thanks."

She put on the headband and sat down. Alec Flint sat down too, but not with Emily Berg.

Alec got a window seat — the best kind — with no one next to him. So he looked out the window and rubbed his hair. He was thinking hard about Ms. Blume. There was last night's thought that she was the anonymous donor, and then this morning's thought that she was maybe a perp. But if she were the anonymous donor, she wouldn't have to disappear. Which left perp. Perps sometimes had to disappear.

But maybe there was a different reason she was gone, though Alec Flint couldn't think of what the reason would be. Dr. Glumsfeld had to know where she was. Or maybe not. Maybe . . . maybe she ran away because she didn't want to marry him! That was a possibility. But then why would she give him the keys to her art room

closets? And why would she leave her dog home alone? Alec thought about it some more. His gut feeling — the feeling that he had deep down in his stomach — told him that running away before the wedding didn't seem right. Not after seeing the icky in-love picture in the newspaper article. But still, he thought the Dr. Glumsfeld thing was important. Somehow the two cases had to be related. Alec just felt it.

Before Alec Flint could figure out how, the school bus pulled up to Laurel Hollows Elementary

East. Alec shuffled off the bus along with the rest of the kids and went to his classroom, hoping he could talk to Gina soon.

Two things happened when Alec got to his desk. One, he discovered that Gina was not there yet. And two, he remembered that it was Teacher Development Day. Actually, he didn't remember, he saw it written on the blackboard in big block letters: *TODAY IS TEACHER DEVELOPMENT DAY.* This meant — as Alec remembered from third and second and first grade, and also from last week when Mrs. Jones passed out a memo about it — that all kids left school before lunchtime, and the teachers stayed to develop things. Alec wasn't exactly sure what they developed, but he figured it was something like new math problems, or plans on how to get bad kids to stop being mean in class. But this also meant that his plans would have to be rearranged for the afternoon. He now had four whole hours free, plus some extra minutes, before he had to be at the museum at 4:30.

Maybe the Bergs would let him play on their lawn again.

Just as Alec started to wonder if Gina knew about the Teacher Development Day situation, she walked in and plopped her stuff down next to him at her desk.

"G'morning, Alec," she said. "Allegra remembered about Teacher Development Day last night and reminded my mom. So she said in case your dad forgot, you can hang out with me this afternoon. I mean, if you want to. I figured we could do some, you know, detective work."

Alec was a little relieved. It meant he wouldn't have to figure out what to do when the dismissal bell rang at 12:17 instead of the lunch one.

"Cool," he said. "My dad did forget. I did too. But that sounds like a good plan. Oh! Also, here, I wrote you a note this morning."

Gina quickly read over the piece of paper that Alec handed her. Then she looked up at him and said, very seriously, "This is getting

119

more and more complicated. We've got to figure it all out."

School went by super fast that day. Mrs. Jones did all the subjects, but really speedy so that instead of forty minutes on math, they only did twenty. And they didn't get to do P.E. because that was usually in the afternoon. So it was just work, work, work all morning long, with a snack break at 10:35. Mrs. Jones passed out celery sticks and peanut butter. Alec Flint liked peanut butter. Not so much celery sticks, but with the peanut butter on them, they weren't half bad.

Before Alec and Gina knew it, the end-of-school bell rang at 12:17, and it was time to meet Mrs. Rossi (the mom — not the other ones) outside of the Willow Street entrance. Alec got his sweatshirt and his backpack. So did Gina.

"Let's go," they both said at the same time.

"Jinx!" said Gina.

"You forgot," said Alec. "I don't *do* jinx."

"Oh, right," said Gina. "I forgot."

Alec and Gina walked out of the classroom and headed to the Willow Street entrance. Gina's mom was there, with Allegra in the car.

"Hey, kiddos," she said, when they came walking out of the building. "How about pizza at Zio Carmine's? I'm in the mood for some mushrooms."

Alec could not believe it. He was having pizza for every meal but breakfast this week! His mom would laugh when she came home and he told her.

"Cool," said Gina. "Okay with you, Alec?"

"Sure," said Alec Flint.

And they drove to Zio Carmine's pizza place, which was called Basta Pizza. Gina told Alec that meant "Enough pizza!" Alec laughed in his head, because that was kind of how he felt. Enough pizza this week!

When they got to the pizza place, Gina jumped

to open the door and she and Alec bounded out of the car. Allegra stayed inside — she was reading again.

"What's she reading?" Alec asked, pointing his head back to the car where Allegra was sitting.

"Karla Kuskin," Gina answered. "She's big into poetry right now. This month it's Karla Kuskin. Last month was Lee Bennett Hopkins. The one before that was Shel Silverstein. I don't know who's next on her list, but she wants to read as many poets as she can by the end of second grade."

"Wow," was all that Alec could think of to say. Gina and her whole family were pretty "wow" to Alec.

Gina had made it to the door of the restaurant with Alec following behind her before Allegra and Mrs. Rossi had a chance to walk out of the parking lot.

"*Ciao*, Zio Carmine!" she shouted as she walked inside. "This is my friend Alec. Can we have pizza?"

"*Ciao, bellina!*" a man behind a pizza counter wearing an apron and some flour on his face shouted back. "For you? Anything! I'll even make it special. Is your *mamma* coming too?"

Gina nodded. And with that, Zio Carmine started twirling uncooked pizza dough in the air.

"Gina," Alec whispered. "What if he drops it?" He'd never seen anyone actually make pizza before, even though he'd eaten it for two meals yesterday. In Alec Flint's experience, pizza either came from a box in the freezer or from a box his dad brought back from a restaurant. Or from the school cafeteria, of course.

Alec watched in awe as Zio Carmine put some spaghetti sauce or something on the dough, and then sprinkled shredded cheese on top. On one section of the pizza pie he put sliced-up meatballs.

"For you, Regina Marie," he said to Gina. By this time Allegra and Mrs. Rossi had walked into the pizza place.

"Oh, thanks, Carmine," Mrs. Rossi said. "You're the best."

"And for you, Cesca," he said as he added mushrooms to another section of the pie.

"And for my little Allegrina — " He added sliced-up tomatoes. "And what about you, Gina's friend?" he said to Alec. "What topping do you like?"

Alec's favorite was pepperoni. Would this man put on pepperoni if he asked? It seemed like it.

"Um, pepperoni, sir," Alec Flint said.

"Pepperoni it is!" said Zio Carmine. "And please, none of this 'sir' business. You can call me Zio Carmine like Gina and Allegra do."

"Uh, okay," said Alec Flint. "Thanks, Zio Carmine." For the life of him, Alec could not figure out why the grown-ups in Gina's family didn't want him to call them by grown-up names. No "Mrs." No "sir." It was all very odd to Alec Flint.

While they were waiting for the pizza to cook, Gina gave Alec a tour of the restaurant, which wasn't so much a restaurant as a little room with a few tables and chairs and a big counter where Zio Carmine made pizza and *zeppole*. Gina also showed Alec the little freezer that had Italian ices inside.

"My favorite is chocolate," she said. "What about you?"

"Um . . ." Alec Flint didn't know what his favorite was. He'd never had Italian ices before. "I like chocolate too," he said. He liked chocolate ice cream, at least, and chocolate candy bars. Not chocolate milk, though. So he wasn't one hundred percent sure if chocolate would be his favorite flavor of Italian ices. Maybe it would be that swirly red-and-blue-and-white one. But he didn't know what the swirly one tasted like, so it seemed safer to say chocolate.

"Gina! Alec!" Gina's mom called to them both. "Pizza's ready."

They went over to where Mrs. Rossi and Allegra were sitting, Allegra trying to eat pizza with one hand and read her book with the other. Mrs. Rossi had set out paper plates and napkins and cups for everyone. Alec sat down in front of the pepperoni slice and looked to see what was inside the cup. Soda! Whoa! Alec was so happy that the *Mission: Impossible* theme song sang itself through his brain. Being friends with Gina? It was a good idea. Definitely had perks.

Mrs. Rossi took a bite of her mushroom pizza and said to Zio Carmine, "Delicious!"

Alec took a bite of his pepperoni pizza. "*Mmm, mine is too*," he said.

"I'll tell the chef," Zio Carmine replied to both of them.

When he walked back behind the counter, Alec whispered to Gina, "Wait, isn't *he* the chef?"

Gina giggled. "Yeah," she said. "He just does that to be funny."

Alec nodded and chewed his pizza slowly. A big idea was forming in his brain. A huge one.

Super huge. Super-gigantic huge. And it all started because of Zio Carmine saying there was a chef when there really wasn't, other than him.

When Alec finished his first slice, he turned to Gina. "What if," he said, "there's no anonymous donor?"

"Huh?" Gina asked, her mouth filled with pizza cheese and meatball.

"Like Zio Carmine and the chef. What if Dr. Glumsfeld is making up that there's an anonymous donor? My dad said that the anonymous donor rich guy is the one who's going to get all the money if no one can find the missing exhibit, and Dr. Glumsfeld won't tell him the name of the guy. What if that's because there *is* no guy?!"

"Huh," Gina said again. "So then where's all the stuff from?"

"I don't know," said Alec. "But maybe it's not real. Like, remember what Mrs. Jones said about the gold? How Christopher Columbus didn't have any, but the exhibit did? I looked online last night and couldn't find out about the gold, but if Mrs. Jones is right, someone could have made up the whole exhibit!"

"Wow," said Gina. "So if we figure out where the stuff is from, will that lead us to the thief?"

"I don't know," said Alec Flint. "But we have to try!"

"So what do we need to do to see if you're right?" Gina asked Alec. "I mean, we don't have any proof right now."

"D'you think your mom would take us to the library before we go to the museum? Then we could find out if Mrs. Jones is right or not. If she is, and there's something big-time wrong with the exhibit, I think we'll have to snoop around the museum."

"Okay," said Gina. "No problem about the library."

Gina spoke to Mrs. Rossi, who said the library was a perfect afternoon trip because she had to do some research there for an article she was writing for the *Herald* anyway. Allegra didn't care, mainly because whatever they did that afternoon, she was just going to read Karla Kuskin.

"Do you know the one about butter?" Allegra asked Alec, the first thing she'd said to him since he'd met her yesterday.

"Um, no," he said, not really sure what she meant, but assuming it was probably a poem.

"Oh," she said. "It's a good one."

"Cool," said Alec, looking around for Gina, who was over with Zio Carmine by the Italian ices freezer.

Before Alec Flint knew it, all the pizza was eaten, the soda was drunk, and, with chocolate Italian ices in hand, he, Gina, Allegra, and Mrs. Rossi were on their way to the library.

Chapter 8

She Thinks Maybe

Once they got into the library, Mrs. Rossi told the kids they could do what they wanted — homework, whatever — but to meet her in the lobby at 3:30 no matter what.

"Remember, Alec has to meet his dad at the museum," Gina told her mom. "Four-thirty at the latest."

"No problem," said Mrs. Rossi. "I have to be at the museum at four o'clock for my meeting with the museum president. And then with Alec's dad at four-thirty. No one can figure out who stole that Christopher Columbus exhibit. I told the paper yesterday that I'd cover it, even before it was such a mystery."

Mrs. Rossi went to the room that held all the microfiche. Allegra sat down in a big cushiony chair with her Karla Kuskin book. And Alec and Gina went to the research area.

"Okay, Alec," Gina said. "So what exactly is it about the gold that we need to find out?"

It made Alec feel good that Gina was asking him instead of trying to be all in charge herself. But it *was* his idea, so that made sense.

"Remember in school when Mrs. Jones asked what Columbus had on his ship?" Alec asked her.

"Yeah," said Gina. "And you said gold coins, and she said no, it was animals and that Columbus was looking for gold in Asia."

"Right," Alec said. "But I went to the Christopher Columbus exhibit the day it opened, before everything got stolen, and there was a big pile of gold coins. And when I read the plaques the morning after everything got stolen, it didn't say anything about animals or finding gold in the Indies or anything. It just said that Columbus took the gold coins on the *Niña* to trade on his first expedition. And that was why I thought maybe the security guard was the perp, because of the gold-coin shape in his pocket. So we need to see if Mrs. Jones is wrong, or if the exhibit is wrong, or what the real story is. If the gold coins are wrong, then maybe there really is no anonymous donor, or if there is, maybe he's a faker."

"Okay," said Gina. "Let's do it!"

Gina found the librarian in charge, who Alec knew a little bit from other times in the library. Her name was Louise Eleanor Allen, and she was happy to help two fourth graders research Christopher Columbus.

"We need to know as much as we can about Christopher Columbus's first voyage to America," Gina said. "And we don't want to read baby books about it. We need the ones that tell you everything. All the details."

"So you're both good readers?" asked Mrs. Allen.

"The best in our class," answered Alec truthfully. "And maybe Roy and Mala too."

"Okay, then," she said, "follow me."

And she led them to the grown-up books in the 900 section of the library.

"Columbus is in the 970s," she said. "Here's a step stool. Let me know if you need any more help or if the books are too hard for you. I'll be at the reference desk."

"Thanks, Mrs. Allen," Alec said as he stepped up on the stool.

"How about you call out the names quietly," Gina said, "and we can decide which ones sound good to pull down? I'll hold them."

"Sure," said Alec. This felt like real sleuthing teamwork.

He softly called out names like *Columbus's Voyage to America* and *Tales of 1492.* He handed both those down to Gina. They decided they

134

didn't want the ones like *Columbus's Influence on the Chicago World's Fair,* which didn't seem to have anything to do with Alec's question about the gold. When Gina had five books stacked in her arms, she said that Alec should come down off the step stool because she couldn't hold any more. He did.

"Okay, we'll just skim," Gina said, "for any mention of gold."

Alec and Gina settled down next to each other at a table and each opened a book. They weren't so much reading as just scanning each page for the letter *g* and then seeing if the word attached to the *g* was *gold*. But even so, it wasn't fast going. The words were little and the pages were big. Sometimes Alec turned pages faster than Gina, and sometimes Gina turned pages faster than Alec.

"Wait!" said Gina. "This might be something!" But before she read it out loud, she shook her head. "Never mind," she said. "It's nothing. Just talking about the golden glow of the sun on the water."

After they flipped a few more pages, Alec said, "I got it!" in the loudest whisper possible. "Here!" he said, and read to Gina, "'Due to the extant letters written by and to Christopher Columbus, it is clear that Columbus promised the Spanish monarchs he would find a trade route to Asia and return with silk, spices, and gold. It's likely he planned to store these goods below deck, in the space vacated by the livestock he kept on board to feed his crew.' I don't know what extant means, and I think maybe monarchs means kings and queens or rich people, but it doesn't even matter. The rest of it is what's important! It says he was looking for gold, and he brought animals. Mrs. Jones was right!"

"Oh my gosh," said Gina. "There's something wrong with the exhibit. Big-time."

"This proves it!" said Alec. "We need to photocopy this page to show to my dad. Do you have a nickel?" Alec thought that the book sounded a little like Dr. Glumsfeld.

Gina Rossi did not have a nickel. Alec Flint did not have a nickel either. He had two singles and two quarters, but those didn't fit into the money slot in the photocopy machine. Only nickels did.

"I bet my mom has one," said Gina.

The two of them walked as quickly as they could without running, because of the no-running-in-the-library rule, to find Gina's mom in the microfiche room. She was there and was feeding coins into the microfiche machine, printing out articles from old newspapers.

"Mom," Gina whispered to her, "can I have a nickel to photocopy something?"

"Sure," said Mrs. Rossi, indicating the pile of coins next to the machine. "Just take one."

Gina took one. She and Alec Flint walked quickly back to the reference room where the photocopy machine was. They couldn't reach the top of the machine, so Alec went and dragged over the step stool that Mrs. Allen gave them to reach the high books. Gina stood on it and tried to figure out how the Columbus book had to go to get the left page photocopied.

"What do you think, Alec?" Gina asked, a little confused. It was the first time Alec had ever seen her look confused about anything.

Alec stepped up on the stool next to Gina.

"How about . . ." he said, placing the page in between little lines that said 8½" and 11". "This should work."

Alec jumped down to get the paper from the tray where it came out.

"Nice!" he said. The page came out perfectly.

Alec folded the paper up small and stuck it in his useful sweatshirt pocket along with his pen that wrote upside down, which — he checked — was still there.

Gina and Alec wanted to be responsible library users, so they put the step stool back where they found it and brought the books they didn't end up looking through to the cart next to Mrs. Allen's desk.

"Thank you very much for your help," said Alec politely.

"My pleasure," said Mrs. Allen.

Alec and Gina started walking back toward the lobby to wait with Allegra.

"Hey, Alec," said Gina. "What does it mean if the exhibit is a fake?"

"I've been thinking," said Alec, "and my brain is saying that it means the robbery is a fake too."

"How could a robbery be a fake?" Gina asked. "I mean, if everything's gone, it was stolen, right?"

"Not sure," said Alec. "It could just be hidden or thrown in the trash so someone could get a lot of money from Emily Berg's dad's insurance company."

"Ohhh," said Gina, looking like she liked this way of thinking.

Then Alec heard shoes *squeak-squeaking* behind him. Gina heard it too, and they both turned around. Allegra was walking toward them.

"Hey, Legs," said Gina.

Allegra glared at her. "Don't *call* me that," she said.

Gina rolled her eyes. "Sorry, Allegra. What's up?"

"It's three twenty-nine. We're supposed to meet Mom in one minute. I didn't want you to get in trouble."

"Thanks," Gina said. Then she turned to Alec. "Let's go meet my mom."

Out in the lobby, Alec, Allegra, and Gina were about to sit down on the couch to wait, when Mrs. Rossi walked in. Alec heard her feet making squeaks on the lobby floor, like Allegra's sneakers, but quieter.

"Hey, kids," she said. "Perfect timing. Who's ready to visit the museum?"

Alec and Gina gave each other private looks. They were ready, but they didn't know what their game plan would be when they got there. They'd have to wing it.

On the way down the library steps, Alec whispered to Gina, "Do you think we'll really crack the Christopher Columbus case?"

"Maybe," Gina said. "I think maybe."

Chapter 9

Not Even Saying Jinx

By the time Alec, Allegra, Gina, and Mrs. Rossi got inside the museum, it was 3:50. Alec Flint still had a whole forty minutes before he had to meet his dad. Mrs. Rossi asked everyone if they wouldn't mind coming with her to the museum president's office for the interview. Nobody minded, so they all followed her up to the third floor, where the offices were. The museum president was there, and she invited Mrs. Rossi in for privacy.

"We'll just wait out here, Mom," Gina said, indicating the hallway. "We'll be quiet, I promise."

"All right, Gi," Mrs. Rossi said. "Stay with your sister."

Mrs. Rossi walked into the museum president's office and closed the door behind her. Alec was getting ready to sit down and wait for the interview to be finished and also was thinking about how they could find out information about Dr. Glumsfeld and the anonymous donor, when Gina said, "Come *on*!"

"What?" said Alec. "We can't go too far or your mom'll get mad. We're supposed to be here when she's done."

"We're not going that far. Just down the hallway. I bet Glumsfeld's office is here too."

"Here!" Allegra said, from farther down the hall. "This one says Glumsfeld on the door."

"Thanks, Legra," Gina said.

She walked quickly down the hall to her sister. Alec Flint followed.

"Okay, Legra," Gina directed. "You keep watch. Alec and I are going inside."

Allegra stood by the door, pretending to read Karla Kuskin. But really, she was keeping an eye on the hallway, making sure no one came near Dr. Glumsfeld's office.

Once they walked in, Alec wasn't sure what to do.

"What are we looking for?" he asked Gina.

"Anything that might be a clue about why the gold coins were in the exhibit, or about Ms. Blume and where she is. I brought my backpack with the other clues, so if you find anything, you can just stick it in there."

"But —" said Alec.

"It's not stealing if we return it," said Gina. "It's just borrowing so we can solve the case."

Alec wasn't thrilled about it, but he said okay anyway.

Then Alec tried to open the drawers in Dr. Glumsfeld's desk. Locked. He looked at the papers on top of the desk. There were some pamphlets that looked like travel brochures. One said,

"*Come to Jamaica!*" Another said, "*Visit Antigua!*" And a third simply said, "*Grand Cayman Islands*" in big blue letters.

"It looks like Dr. Glumsfeld is planning a trip," Alec said out loud. He brought the clues over to Gina's backpack.

Gina didn't respond; she was looking through a pile of papers on the floor next to the couch.

Before Alec dropped the clues in the bag, he saw a scrap of paper sticking out of the Grand

Cayman Islands brochure. It looked like a really short to-do list. In messy handwriting it said:

TO DO

1) SECURE PASSPORTS

2) FIND PLACE TO HIDE KAREN

Then at the very bottom of the list it said, without a number next to it:

MUMMIES.

"Hey, Gina?" Alec asked. "What do you know about mummies?"

"Well, I know that they're dead people all wrapped up in stuff that looks like toilet paper," she answered. "And that they're from olden days in Egypt."

"Why do you think Dr. Glumsfeld wrote that on his to-do list?"

"Dunno," Gina said. "Maybe he likes them."

"Yeah, maybe," Alec agreed.

He dropped the sticky note in Gina's backpack. Then he pulled it out again.

"Wait," Alec Flint said. "Do you know what Ms. Blume's first name is?"

"Something with a *K*," she answered. "When we were in the art room, all her books said K. Blume in them. Wait. It's on that newspaper article."

Gina pulled the framed article out of her bag. "Karen," she said to Alec, after reading for a second. "Her name is Karen Anne Blume."

"Look at this sticky note," he said. "Could she be the Karen? Could he be hiding her somewhere?"

"Oh my gosh," said Gina. "Do you think he kidnapped her? And is taking her away to one of those islands? And that's why he needs her passport?"

"I don't know," said Alec. "Let's keep looking."

He kept rifling through the papers on Dr. Glumsfeld's desk. But nothing looked that important.

"Hey!" Gina said, from her pile of papers on the floor. "Another sticky-note list!"

Alec looked over Gina's shoulder. The list said:

1) TELESCOPE
2) GOLD LEAF
3) BOOK FROM KAREN
4) SWORDS FROM COSTUME STORE (BORROW)
5)

The list wasn't finished.

"Why does he need a book from Ms. Blume?" Gina asked.

"Dunno," said Alec.

Then Allegra, the ever-present timekeeper, yelled into the room, "Guys, Alec has to meet his dad in three minutes! And he probably doesn't want to get in trouble for being late!"

Alec looked at Gina. "I gotta make a run for it so my dad doesn't get mad."

"I'll run with you," Gina said. "Maybe there are clues in the empty exhibit hall."

"Legs?" Gina had turned toward her sister. "Can you tell Mom that Alec and I ran down to the exhibit hall to meet Alec's dad?"

"Sure," said Allegra, going back to reading. "But don't *call* me that."

"Sorry," said Gina.

Then she and Alec took off. Alec wasn't sure if there was a no-running rule in the museum, but he really didn't care. Being late was a bad thing as far as Officer Flint was concerned. It made him think that terrible things had happened to you. So Alec was never late. Except to school, but that didn't count, since his dad was usually the one taking him there. According to Officer Flint, sometimes that just couldn't be helped.

Alec shouldn't have worried. When they got to the exhibit hall, Officer Flint was talking to some people in the corner. He waved his hand when Alec and Gina walked in and then went back to talking. Officer Sanchez, who was Officer Flint's partner, waved to Alec too.

"Let's walk around and you tell me what used to be in the exhibit," Gina said to Alec.

So he showed her around. Alec Flint led Gina to the podium where the telescope used to be. He told her about Emily Berg dropping the telescope.

"I was worried it was going to break," Alec told Gina. "But it didn't."

As Alec said the words, a thought popped into his brain, and he wasn't even rubbing his hair. Actually it was two thoughts. The first thought was that plastic didn't break, glass did. And the second thought was that there was no plastic in 1492. This was another problem with the exhibit, like the gold.

"Hey, Gina," Alec said. "There's something wrong. No plastic in fourteen ninety-two. The telescope see-through part should've broken when Emily dropped it. It must not have been made of glass."

"Weird," said Gina.

Alec pulled out his detective notebook and wrote down: *telescope — no plastic in 1492.* He ripped out the page and dropped it in with the other clues in Gina's backpack.

Then they walked to the glass case that used to hold the Captain's Log, the book that had looked like it was made of an old shoe. He showed Gina the pictures of the maps and the curlicue handwriting still on the walls.

"Hey," Gina said. "This is in Italian!"

"Ooh, what does it say?" asked Alec Flint.

"That page is called 'Our First Look at America,' and that other one is called 'Close Up: The American Shoreline,'" she answered. "Do you want me to read the whole thing?"

Something about those labels seemed weird to Alec. He ran his hand over his spiky hair. *Come on,* he said to himself. His brain was sounding like Gina! And then Alec got it. *America.*

"Gina!" he said. "Christopher Columbus would never write the word *America*! It wasn't invented yet."

"No way," said Gina. "More fakes? This is crazy! What else is there to look at?"

But then the men in the corner with Officer Flint started getting loud. There was someone Alec didn't know who was yelling at Dr. Glumsfeld.

"You must tell us the name of the anonymous donor, Theodore!" the voice was saying.

Alec and Gina looked over at the corner. Officer Flint looked over at Alec and Gina. He whispered something to Fernando-call-me-Frank, who was there too. Then the possible-perp security guard came over to Alec and Gina.

"Hello," he said to Alec, giving him the fish-eye — his eyes were creepy like the ones on a dead

153

fish floating at the top of a fishbowl. "Your father says that you two might be better off keeping yourselves busy in the room across the hallway where they started to set up the sarcophaguses for the Egypt exhibit. Take a look around if you want. We can keep an eye on you through the security camera."

Gina shrugged and then said, "Okay, thanks."

Alec looked at her with big eyes, but she mouthed to him, not making even one sound, "Mummies go in sarcophaguses."

Alec got it. He and Gina followed Call-me-Frank into the mummy room across the hall. As he was leaving, Frank pulled something out of his back pocket. *Cripes,* thought Alec Flint, *it's the gold coin!* He was getting ready to run for his dad. Only then Frank unwrapped the coin. It was chocolate candy. The kind that looks like a gold coin but isn't. Alec checked and there was nothing else in Call-me-Frank's back pocket. Well, at least that narrowed things down. Call-me-Frank was not the perp. Or if he was, there was even less proof about it than before.

"I don't think it's the security guard," Alec whispered to Gina. "The thing I thought was a coin was just candy."

"Oh," said Gina. "Well, that's at least one possible suspect we don't have to think about anymore."

"Yeah," said Alec. "Hey, what do you think we should look for in the mummies?"

"I don't know," Gina said, checking out the room.

"Maybe we should look at all of our evidence," Alec suggested.

Gina shrugged. "Sure," she said. And she sat down. Alec Flint sat down too. He and Gina started pulling things out of her backpack. They had a pretty big pile. There was the newspaper article in the frame, the note from Ms. Blume saying she was going to meet someone with the initials of TG, the travel pamphlets, the two sticky notes from Dr. Glumsfeld's office, the note Alec wrote about the telescope. Alec looked at the clues and realized something was missing. He pulled out his detective note-book and wrote on a piece of paper, *The Captain's Log — no America,* and added that to the collection. But there was still something else. . . . Then Alec remembered the photocopy about the gold coins that he'd stuck in his sweat-shirt pocket. He pulled that out and added it to the pile too.

Alec Flint and Gina Rossi looked at the clues. Then Gina picked up the note saying Ms. Blume was going to meet TG.

"Did you hear the guy in there call someone Theodore?" she asked Alec.

"Yeah," he said. "The guy was talking to Dr. Glumsfeld," he answered.

"The newspaper called him Sanford Theodore Glumsfeld, but I thought he probably goes by his middle name." Gina said. "I bet *he's* the TG Ms. Blume met on Thursday at four o'clock, which is right after the last time anyone at school saw her."

"That makes sense, kind of," said Alec Flint. "I mean, they *are* getting married."

"Still," Gina said. "I think it's important."

Alec knew what to do. He whipped out his detective notebook again and started making a list.

1) Dr. Glumsfeld and Ms. Blume are getting married on Saturday.

2) Ms. Blume went to meet TG (probably Dr. Glumsfeld) at 4:00 on Thursday, and no one at East has seen or heard from her since. She didn't pick up her mail, and she left her dog home alone.

Then he and Gina kept looking at the clues. Alec pulled out the to-do list Gina found in Dr.

Glumsfeld's office, the one with the telescope on it. Plus, he pulled out the two notes he'd ripped from his detective notebook.

"Gina!" he said, super excited. "I think Dr. Glumsfeld is the one who faked the exhibit! Look! On his to-do list it says that he needs to get a telescope — only he got the wrong kind, one with plastic, not glass. And it says he's going to borrow swords from a costume store, and well, I don't know what gold leaf is, but 'get the book from Karen' — do you think that means Ms. Blume is the one who made the Captain's Log?"

"Oh my gosh!" said Gina. "Her handwriting is all loopy like that — I remember from last week in art when she wrote my name on the back of the piece of paper she gave me for shape drawing!"

"That means," said Alec Flint — at least, this is what he thought it meant — "that there really is no anonymous donor! It really *is* just like with Zio Carmine and the chef — Dr. Glumsfeld is the anonymous donor, only not really, because he's a faker."

As Alec Flint added all this stuff to his list, he got a sad feeling in his stomach. "You know what this means if we're right, Gina," he said. "It means that Ms. Blume is part of it. She made the book. And she was going to marry a criminal. And I bet the whole fake exhibit is what's locked in the art room closets — that's why Emily Berg saw Dr. Glumsfeld at East on Sunday."

Alec thought again about the green not-patterned vase he'd made in Ms. Blume's class and about the ballerina she drew for Emily. As Alec was thinking, he was staring straight at the sarcophagus in front of him. It looked like there was something inside trying to get out! He could see a glint of something sparkly slicing a big rect-angle through the wood.

"Gina?" he said. "Gina? Are you seeing what I'm seeing?"

"If you're seeing tons of mummy cases, I am. 'Cause that's what I'm seeing."

"Not the mummy cases, the part of a rectangle on the side of this one."

Gina looked at the part of a rectangle.

"Oh my gosh," she said. "It's like it's appearing! Like the mummy in there is drawing it."

Alec gulped. "I don't think it's the mummy. I think it might be . . ."

Gina and Alec both stood up at the same time and ran over to the sarcophagus.

"Ms. Blume!" they both shouted together. Gina didn't even say "jinx."

They heard a thumping coming from the sarcophagus. Then Alec saw Dr. Glumsfeld walking quickly out of the ex–Christopher Columbus exhibit hall.

"Gina!" he said. "You've gotta follow Dr. Glumsfeld. Don't let him get away! I have to get my dad!"

Gina ran out of the mummy room, down the hallway after Dr. Glumsfeld. Alec ran out of the mummy room, across the hallway to his father.

"Dad!" he yelled as he got into the former Christopher Columbus exhibit hall. "Dad! Ms. Blume, my art teacher, is in a sarcophagus, and Dr. Glumsfeld is the perp!"

"What?!" said Officer Flint.

"I'm serious, Dad. For real. No joke."

Alec Flint pulled his father back across the hallway to the sarcophagus with three-quarters of a rectangle carved into it.

"In *here*," Alec said. "Ms. Blume's in *here*."

Officer Flint knocked on the wood of the sarcophagus. A very muffled voice answered him.

"Cripes!" he said. "You're right, Alec, there's someone in there."

He radioed for the security guards at the museum, who came with a crowbar. Then he turned back to Alec. "And *what* was it you were saying about Dr. Glumsfeld?" Officer Flint asked his son.

"He's the perp," Alec said. "He faked the whole thing, and there's no anonymous donor. Also, he's marrying Ms. Blume this weekend."

"The woman in the sarcophagus?" Officer Flint asked.

Alec nodded.

"All right, Al," said Officer Flint. "I'm not sure how you figured all this out, or even if I completely understand what you're talking about. But I guess that can wait for now because you're definitely right about someone being trapped in that sarcophagus. I'll believe you about the rest. Let's see if we can stop Dr. Glumsfeld before he leaves the museum."

Officer Flint radioed the security guards again. But he didn't really have to, because just as he was giving the message to stop Dr. Glumsfeld from leaving the museum, Gina showed up with a whole parade behind her. That parade included Dr. Glumsfeld, whose arm was held behind his back by Alfred Berg, who was followed by Emily Berg. And behind Emily was Mrs. Rossi, Allegra, and the woman who Alec had glimpsed when Mrs. Rossi went to interview her — the president of the museum.

"I demand to know the meaning of this!" Dr. Glumsfeld was shouting.

"Al?" Officer Flint looked to his son. "You'd better explain now or Mr. Berg could be in trouble for grabbing the curator of the Christopher Columbus exhibit for no reason and twisting his arm."

Alec turned to Gina. "You want to tell it?" he asked her. "Or should I?"

"Let's both," she answered.

So Alec started. He pulled out his detective notebook and gathered up the pile of clues, which he handed to his father.

"You see," he said. "It all started when I thought Fernando the security guard was the perp, the morning we came here that I was late for school."

"But he's not," said Officer Flint.

"But I'm not," repeated Fernando, who was one of the security guards prying open the sarcophagus.

"He has an airtight alibi," said Officer Flint.

164

"I know he's not," said Alec Flint. "But I thought he was. So I decided that I had to prove it and help everyone solve this case. Only I needed a sleuthing partner, so I asked Gina."

"But," said Gina, "I already had a mystery to solve, which was where Ms. Blume had disappeared to."

"So," said Alec, "we decided we'd solve both cases. And we looked around in the art room —"

"Wait a minute," said Officer Flint. "You looked around in the art room? Do you mean you snooped? You searched without permission?"

"Well, yes," admitted Alec Flint, his stomach feeling a little marshmallowy.

"We'll talk about that later, Al," said Officer Flint. "You're not supposed to snoop in other people's things without a search warrant. But for now, continue."

Alec Flint gulped. Then he continued. "Anyway, so we found the wedding announcement for Dr. Glumsfeld and Ms. Blume, and then Emily Berg told me she saw someone who walked and talked like Dr. Glumsfeld in the art room hallway at school when she was practicing for ballet. So then Gina and I thought the two cases might be related."

"And also," Gina said, "we found a piece of paper that said Ms. Blume was going to meet TG at four o'clock on Thursday, which is right after the last time anyone at school saw her. And we figured out today that TG must be Theodore Glumsfeld."

"Yeah," said Alec. "And then Mrs. Jones said that Columbus didn't have any gold coins on his ship. So then I knew that either the exhibit was wrong or Mrs. Jones was wrong. Only I couldn't find any information online."

"But today," said Gina, "we went to the library, where we found out that Mrs. Jones was right, and the exhibit was wrong."

"Also, we had pizza," said Alec. "Where because of what Zio Carmine said, I got the idea that maybe there was no anonymous donor. And then we came to the museum. And we looked in Dr. Glumsfeld's office — sorry, Dad."

Alec Flint looked down at his sneaker toes, but Gina wasn't looking at hers.

"Right," she said, "and we found these lists of stuff to do and also travel brochures."

"And then, when we came down to the exhibit, I realized the telescope had to be a fake because it didn't break when Emily dropped it. I remembered the lesson about plastic bouncing and glass breaking, from the water when you were coughing," said Alec. "And then Gina read the Italian on the Captain's Log, and the word *America* was in it, so we knew that was a fake too."

"Then," said Gina, "we came in here, and Alec looked at the list of stuff Dr. Glumsfeld wanted to get, plus the list of things in the exhibit, and he figured it all out. That there was definitely no anonymous donor, and Dr. Glumsfeld faked the whole thing."

"Cripes!" said Officer Flint. "And then he'd get all the insurance money! Why didn't I think of that?"

Alec and Gina shrugged.

"Oh yeah," said Alec. "And then we saw something shiny cutting through the mummy sarcophagus, and we figured that somehow Ms. Blume got stuck in there, because of Dr. Glumsfeld writing himself a note about mummies. And also, we think she might be a little bit of a perp too. For faking the Captain's Log."

"I always hated smarty-pants kids," said Dr. Glumsfeld.

By this point, Fernando-call-me-Frank and the two other security guards had pried the lid off the sarcophagus. Ms. Blume climbed out, right into the crowd of people.

"Everything the children just said is right," she cried, "but I'm not a thief or a forger, really.

I made the book for Theo because I loved him. I thought he wanted to keep it in our living room for fun. And when I heard about his scheme, I argued with him. And he took my art closet keys and trapped me in the museum. He's been moving me around from room to room, locking me in storerooms and exhibits ever since. I'm so glad you both found me!"

Ms. Blume ran over to Alec and Gina and hugged them. She kissed Alec on his cheek, and he turned bright red. He did not like kisses. Especially from people who were not related to him. Come to think of it, he didn't even like related-to-him kisses very much.

"Pete," Alec's dad said to Officer Sanchez, "why don't you cuff Glumsfeld and take him down to the station? I'll deal with the rest of the mess here."

Earlier, during Alec and Gina's story, Pete Sanchez had called for backup, and as Ms. Blume had emerged from the sarcophagus, the museum began to fill with police officers. One of them went with Ms. Blume to the art room, where she unlocked the closets and found the entire fake Christopher Columbus exhibit. And also Dr. Glumsfeld's teddy bear, which he'd left there for safekeeping. The gold leaf, which, Alec and Gina learned, was cheapo sheets of gold Dr. Glumsfeld had put on tin coins to make everyone think they were gold through and through, was what had been shiny when they peeked in the closet. The bear had been what was furry. Plus, it turned out that Dr. Glumsfeld wasn't really a curator at all — he was a faker about that too. He'd tricked the museum!

Throughout all of this, Francesca Rossi was writing as quickly as she could. "What a story!" she said. "The newspaper's going to love this one. An art fraud and missing persons case solved by two fourth graders!"

"And me, a little," said Allegra. "I kept a lookout and did the timekeeping. And I found his office door."

"With the help of a second grader," said Mrs. Rossi.

"And with the help of Emily Berg," Alec said, pulling Emily toward him and Gina. "She made the telescope bounce and told me about Dr. Glumsfeld at school."

"And she kicked Dr. Glumsfeld in the shin when I was chasing him and knocked him over," Gina added.

"You did?" Alec asked Emily.

"You did?" echoed Officer Flint.

"She did," said Alfred Berg.

"Yeah," said Emily. "I was practicing a grand jeté for my dad. Not like I do one in the ballet show, but Cinderella does. So I was showing him, and — *bam!* — I jetéd into the weirdo museum guy, and he fell. He tried to hit me, which is when

172

my dad grabbed his arm, and Gina told us he was a bad guy."

"Wow." Alec Flint smiled. Two cases were solved, and it turned out that Emily Berg might not be such a bad sleuth after all.

Francesca Rossi had called the *Laurel Hollows Herald*, and a photographer came to take pictures of the empty exhibit hall and the sarcophagus, and Alec, Gina, Allegra, and Emily.

The Laurel Hollows Herald

MUSEUM MYSTERY SOLVED

ALEC FLINT AND GINA ROSSI SOLVE CASE

And even though Alec and Gina helped to put a criminal behind bars and saved Alfred Berg's company from paying big bucks, and even though their pictures were on the front page of the newspaper, they still got in trouble for snooping around in other people's property. Gina got double in trouble for running off in the museum and not telling her mom or staying with her sister. For their punishment, they were going to have to spend a whole weekend cleaning up the art room. With one break allowed, to see Emily as a happy tree in the *Cinderella* ballet. But they didn't think the punishment was really that bad, because they'd be together. Plus, who knew what they'd find in there? It might just lead to another mystery.

Alec Flint certainly hoped so.

Page 34

Dear Allegra,

My class is sooo boring.

Page 49

Gina,

The thing about the museum is this: I saw one of the security guards with something in his pocket that looked like a gold coin. And gold coins were one of the things missing from the stolen exhibit. So I think Fernando the guard might be the thief. Can you think of a way we can get into the museum to sleuth?

— Alec

Alec,

Maybe we could just ask one of our parents to take us to the museum — we could say it's for a school project or something. Maybe we could do that tomorrow? Can you meet me in the art room after school today? I bet there are clues here for the Ms. Blume mystery.

— Gina

Page 50
I would, but I'd miss the bus.

My mom will take you home. Deal?

Yes.

Page 52
Alec,

Pay attention! This might be helpful for our case.

— Gina

Page 56
I know there were gold coins in the exhibit that got stolen. We have to get back to the museum.

Page 57

Tomorrow. Don't worry.

Hungry?

Page 68

I have a plan on how to get into the art room. Meet me there five minutes after the dismissal bell.

— Gina

P.S. I forgive you for not sitting with me at lunch.

Pages 113-114

'Morning Gina,

I think our two cases might be connected somehow. Emily Berg says she saw Dr. Glumsfeld, the museum guy, in the school hallway on Sunday right near the art room. I wonder what it means. Let's talk at lunch.

— Alec

Author's Note

Even though this book about Alec and his friends is fiction, all of the information about Christopher Columbus is fact. Christopher Columbus was born in Italy, where even today there are streets, hotels, and an entire airport named after him, using the Italian version of his name, Cristoforo Colombo. Columbus grew up in Italy and most likely didn't go to school for very long. Some historians say he started working on boats when he was only ten.

VENICE

CHRISTOFORO COLOMBO
GENOA

FLORENCE

ROME

ITALY

When Columbus was older, he became a sailor and an explorer. His goal was to find trade routes through the seas from Europe to Asia. His trips were sponsored by the Spanish monarchs, Queen Isabella and King Ferdinand, who eventually made him an admiral. He is recognized and honored in Spain, just like in Italy, but there they call him Cristóbal Colón.

Christopher Columbus had three ships in his fleet — the *Niña*, the *Pinta*, and the *Santa María*. According to his journals, which historians still have today, the *Niña* was Columbus's favorite. And it's true that he brought animals with him from Europe to the New World. Records say that Columbus had horses, cows, pigs, and chickens aboard the *Niña* and kept them hung in slings so that they wouldn't break their legs from the rolling of the sea.

Columbus made four voyages to the New World — the first in 1492, the second in 1493, the third in 1498, and the last in 1502. It wasn't until 1498 that Columbus reached the mainland of America. Columbus, along with his brothers Bartolomeo and Diego, ruled a small community of Spaniards on the island of Hispaniola, and Columbus is often criticized for his poor treatment of the Native Americans he encountered there. After a while, people in the New World turned against the Columbus brothers and sent them back to Spain in chains. There, Christopher Columbus was stripped of his title, Admiral of the Ocean Sea. Along with his son Fernando and his brother Bartolomeo, Columbus made one final voyage to the New World in search of the Strait of Malacca and the Indian Ocean, but by that point Vasco de Gama had sailed around the Cape of Good Hope in Africa and found a real trade route to Asia, and Amerigo Vespucci had laid claim to the discovery of the new continents Columbus had failed to realize he happened upon until it was too late.

In writing this book, I researched Christopher Columbus — and also recalled things I'd been taught about him in elementary school, middle school, and high school. If you want to learn more about Columbus, there is a lot written about him on the Web, as well as some wonderful books about his life. I specifically recommend *Follow the Dream: The Story of Christopher Columbus* by Peter Sis; *Meet Christopher Columbus* by James T. De Kay; and, for anyone interested in a fictionalized account of Columbus's life, *Christopher Columbus: Young Explorer* by Kathleen Kudlinski.

Christopher Columbus is a very controversial historical figure, but one who most certainly caused big changes in the world through his explorations. I hope you enjoyed reading this book about him as much as I enjoyed writing it.

— *Jill Santopolo*
New York, NY

Acknowledgments

Alec Flint would still be a pile of pages on my bedroom floor if it weren't for the help, support, and encouragement of many wonderful people: Lisa Sandell, who shaped this book with her kind heart and editorial wisdom; Jodi Reamer, who looked at a twenty-page story and saw a novel; Michael Stearns, whose smart, unerring advice made this narrative work; the team at Scholastic who embraced Alec — Ed Masessa, Elizabeth Parisi, Kristina Albertson, Susan Schultz, and everyone else who had a hand in bringing this story from manuscript to finished book; Eleanor Coufos, who was the very first person to read about Alec; my friends and family who gave me the time, space, and encouragement to write; and my teachers at Hewlett Elementary School — especially Mrs. Joan Jones, Mrs. Margot Hall, and Mrs. Ayala Rosen — whose Do Nows and classroom rules made their way into this story. I thank you all so very much.

About the Author

Jill Santopolo is not a super-sleuth-in-training, though she is particularly good at walking quickly and quietly through the streets of New York City, where she lives. She recently received her MFA in writing for Children and Young Adults from Vermont College, and now spends most of her time reading books, writing books, and editing some other ones. You can visit her online at www.jillsantopolo.com.